CHRISTIANITY
and the
SUPERNATURAL

CHRISTOPHER
BREARLEY

Published by Zaccmedia
www.zaccmedia.com
info@zaccmedia.com

Published February 2014
Copyright © 2014 Christopher Brearley

ISBN: 978-1-909824-13-3

British Library Cataloguing-in-Publication Data
A catalogue record for this book is available from the British Library

CONTENTS

INTRODUCTION

Initially I was hesitant to write a book on so complex and emotive a subject as the supernatural. I am very aware that certain things transcend our comprehension, and as a result are subject to wide differences of interpretation. What is the possibility or probability of something occurring that is beyond what is natural or normal? Do we believe in spiritual gifts and spiritual warfare today? Is it possible to have any true insight into life after death? Or are we captivated by the world of science and technology to such a degree that we eradicate any sense of the mysterious from our lives?

Some people refuse to believe in the supernatural in any way, shape or form. They would accept that anything beyond the so-called natural or normal should be treated as a mere figment of the imagination. If we accept a philosophy which excludes the supernatural, this is what we shall believe.

There is a second group who possess an unhealthy fascination for the supernatural. That is why in many Christian bookshops you will find that numerous books focus on feelings rather than sound Bible doctrine or theology. Curiosity often stirs people to respond to anything out of the ordinary. Hence, their insatiable appetite for new and exciting experiences will cause them to seek and to attempt things that wiser people would avoid or be more cautious of.

A third group includes those who are afraid of anything supernatural or unusual. It is a strange, unfamiliar world to which they cannot accustom themselves. They are adamant about having everything under their complete control and do not want to be disturbed. As a consequence they lack spiritual zeal and fall into the serious error of what Scripture calls 'quenching the Spirit' (see 1 Thessalonians 5:19).

How, then, should we react to the supernatural? That is the crucial question, and the answer is not always straightforward. Most likely it will be impossible for me to adopt any position without upsetting someone. Personal prejudices and denominationalism can often influence our decisions and lead us astray.

It is so easy to see our own interpretation of Scripture as being the only acceptable one. Therefore we can react irrationally, sometimes ungraciously, and in an unbiblical way that leads to acrimonious controversy and bitter division. That is why it is essential to tackle all modern popular philosophical issues with an open mind and in the light of Scripture. There is no substitute for the supremacy and sufficiency of God's Word.

Great care must always be taken not to pluck texts out of context so as to justify our own ideas or traditions. This I have strived to do. I do not claim to have a monopoly on the truth and I readily accept that many issues are open to differences of interpretation. This is not necessarily a bad thing, for debate is often helpful when searching for the truth.

Space inevitably forbids the covering of every detail of such a vast and important subject. For this reason there will be some important omissions. Even so, my heartfelt prayer is that God will use my efforts to provide a useful insight into how we should respond to the supernatural. May our ears be opened to listen to what the Spirit is saying to us!

CHAPTER 1

THE PERSON AND WORK OF THE HOLY SPIRIT

From every standpoint, Christianity is a supernatural phenomenon. For instance, the coming of the Holy Spirit at Pentecost endowed the Church with divine power, and without that power nothing worthwhile could have been accomplished (Acts 2). But who, or what, is the Holy Spirit? Is the same power that came at Pentecost available to us today? Can Christians experience a baptism of the Spirit after and in addition to their conversion? And how can we know?

It would be a mistake to believe that the Holy Spirit was inactive prior to Pentecost. We see Jesus performing his ministry in the power of the Holy Spirit (Luke 4:14). The Holy Spirit had descended upon him at the time of his baptism and had guided him in the wilderness (Luke 3:22; 4:1). Was Jesus not, indeed, conceived by the power of the Holy Spirit, resulting in what we now call the virgin birth (Luke 1:35)?

The references to the Holy Spirit in the Old Testament are few in comparison to the New Testament. There are, however, several accounts in the Old Testament of how the Spirit guided the leaders and prophets of Israel. In the book of Judges we see how the Spirit guided such men as Othniel (3:10); Gideon (6:34); Jephthah (11:29); and Samson (13:25), thus giving them success. Later in Israel's history, that was the reason for David's success. Samuel anointed him to be king, 'and from that day on the Spirit of the LORD came upon David in power' (1 Samuel 16:13).

Throughout the Bible it is clear that the Holy Spirit is co-equal, co-existent and co-eternal with the Father and the Son. 1 Corinthians 8:6 reveals 'there is but one God, the Father'; then John 1:1–3 places beyond dispute that the Son is also God; while Acts 5:3,4 does the same concerning the Holy Spirit. All three are God. In spite of that, Christians accept the fact that the Father, Son and Holy Spirit are distinguishable. Scripture repeatedly reveals that the Father is not the Son; the Son is not the Father; and neither of them is the Holy Spirit.

All three were present, but in different forms, at the baptism of Jesus (Matthew 3:16, 17). Jesus promised his disciples that he will ask the Father, and he will give them another (note another, not the same) Helper. This Helper is the Holy Spirit (John 14:16,17). A distinction is made in the command to baptize people in the name of the Father and of the Son and of the Holy Spirit (Matthew 28:19). Furthermore, to emphasize this threefold character of God, the apostle Paul wrote: 'May the grace of the Lord Jesus Christ, and the love of God, and the fellowship of the Holy Spirit be with you all' (2 Corinthians 13:14).

Does, therefore, the Bible teach a polytheistic concept of God? Are there three Gods? That is, the Father is God, the Son is God, and the Holy Spirit is God; three separate and distinct gods? Or is there only one God?

If all this sounds puzzling, don't worry. When we come to

try to explain what is termed the doctrine of the Trinity, we are at a loss. Our finite minds are unable to fully comprehend the infinite God. How can three be one and one three? It has been aptly said that if you try to understand the majestic mystery of the Trinity you will lose your mind, and if you deny it you will lose your soul. Certainly it is a sin to doubt or deny the existence of the Trinity, but it is not a sin to admit our ignorance of God's mysterious ways. Indeed, if we knew all there was to know about God, he would be reduced to human dimensions. He would be much too small.

What is clear from Scripture is that God is one and there is no other (Deuteronomy 6:4; Isaiah 45:22). At the same time we are compelled to acknowledge that God exists eternally in three distinct persons, each indwelling the other and each possessing, not in part, but completely, the infinite substance of the one divine being. Hence, all must equally be the central object of our love and worship.

In this chapter, our study of the Holy Spirit falls under six main headings: first, his personality; second, his deity; third, his work; fourth, the gifts he bestows; fifth, the fullness of the Spirit in the life of the believer; and finally, the fruitfulness of the Spirit.

THE PERSONALITY OF THE SPIRIT

The Bible teaches that the Spirit is not merely a power but a divine person, just like the Father and the Son. But we must realize that the term 'person' is only used for convenience. In human language it is appropriate because the Spirit possesses and performs the qualities of a person. That is why Jesus refers to the Holy Spirit as 'him' or 'he', not 'it' (John 14:17). Clearly, this is indicative of a personal being rather than an impersonal force. Moreover, the Bible ascribes many personal attributes to him.

The Spirit speaks: *'He who has an ear, let him hear what the Spirit says to the churches'* (Revelation 2:7). The Spirit told Philip to walk beside the chariot of the Ethiopian eunuch (Acts 8:29). He spoke to Peter, when the deputation from Cornelius arrived at Joppa, and told him to go and present the gospel of Christ to a Gentile audience (Acts 10:19,20). The Holy Spirit said to the church at Antioch: *'Set apart for me Barnabas and Saul for the work to which I have called them'* (Acts 13:2). When Paul and his companions attempted to go into Bithynia, the Spirit prevented them (Acts 16:7). The book of Acts, as we have seen, again and again recognizes the Spirit personally speaking to the minds of Christ's servants.

The Spirit may be stubbornly resisted, as Stephen accused the Jewish leaders and their forefathers of doing. They did this repeatedly by their unresponsiveness and resistance to God's revelation and by intentionally persecuting, even killing, those who were inspired by the Holy Spirit. This reached its climax in the violent murder of the Righteous One himself (Acts 7:51,52).

The Spirit is affected by the way people behave. Because of people's ingratitude and rejection, even after having done so much for them, the Holy Spirit was grieved (Isaiah 63:10). Surely, since he is holy, he is always grieved by any form of unholiness. It is to reinforce this point that Paul tells us not to grieve the Holy Spirit of God (Ephesians 4:30).

Neither should the Holy Spirit be insulted. This is done by one who has *'trampled the Son of God under foot'* and has also *'insulted the Spirit of grace'* (Hebrews 10:29). *'If we deliberately keep on sinning after we have received the knowledge of truth, no sacrifice for sins is left, but only a fearful expectation of judgment and of raging fire that will consume the enemies of God'* (vv. 26,27). People who sin intentionally and who keep on doing so can never say that they have sinned in ignorance.

Jesus emphasizes what a vital error it is not to recognize the work of the Spirit. *'And so I tell you, every sin and blasphemy will be forgiven men, but the blasphemy against the Spirit will not be forgiven. Anyone who speaks a word against the Son of Man will be forgiven, but anyone who speaks against the Holy Spirit will not be forgiven, either in this age or in the age to come'* (Matthew 12:31,32). To blaspheme against the Holy Spirit is the only sin that can never be forgiven. Why not? It is because such people have hearts that have become so hardened that they refuse to pay any attention to the prompting, pleading and warning voice of the Spirit, and have placed themselves on the road that leads to eternal death. Now, if any person is ever worried that they may have committed the unpardonable sin, we can confidently assure them that they have not, because if they had they would not be concerned about it.

None of the above characteristics, and there are others, can be attributed to an impersonal force. But what biblical proof is there that this personal being, the Spirit, is also a supreme being?

THE DEITY OF THE SPIRIT

The Bible teaches that the Spirit is not only a person, the third person of the Trinity: he is God. For example, Peter said, *'Ananias, how is it that Satan has so filled your heart that you have lied to the Holy Spirit...?'* and then in the next verse, he states as a fact: *'You have not lied to men but to God'* (Acts 5:3,4). Peter speaks of the Holy Spirit and God interchangeably, and so it necessarily follows that the Spirit is indeed God.

The attributes ascribed to the Spirit are further evidence of his interpersonal relationship within the Godhead.

- He is called the Holy Spirit: This is the definitive attribute of God. He is inherently holy and so has the right to such a title.

- He is called the eternal Spirit (Hebrews 9:14): This means that there never was a time when he did not exist and neither can he die.

- He is omnipotent (that is, all-powerful): The angel Gabriel leaves Mary in no doubt that the Holy Spirit will come upon her, and the power of the Most High will overshadow her. Hence, the baby born to her will be holy, and he will be called the Son of God (Luke 1:35). Clearly, her conception will arise from a divine, not a human, action.

- He is omniscient (that is, he knows everything): *'The Spirit searches all things, even the deep things of God. For who among men knows the thoughts of a man except the man's spirit within him? In the same way no-one knows the thoughts of God except the Spirit of God'* (1 Corinthians 2:10b,11). There are things which are so personal that no one knows them except an individual's own spirit. Likewise the Spirit, who is one in essence with the Father and the Son, is the only person who can lead us into an intimate knowledge of God. He searches everything and nothing escapes his attention.

- He is omnipresent (that is, existing everywhere simultaneously): There is no part of heaven, earth or the universe that is not occupied by the Spirit. *'Where can I go from your Spirit? Where can I flee from your presence?'* (Psalm 139:7). King David knew that no matter where he fled, however remote, he could not flee from the presence of God's Spirit. No mere creature can be in two or more places at once.

THE WORK OF THE SPIRIT

The Bible further confirms the deity of the Spirit through his divine works. Was not the Spirit active in the work of creation? (Genesis 1:2; Job 33:4). All Scripture is breathed out by God (2 Timothy 3:16), the source of which is the Holy Spirit (2 Peter 1:21). Christ was raised from the dead by the Spirit (Romans 8:11). It is the Holy Spirit who convinces men of sin (John 16:8). He teaches us and guides us into all truth (John 14:26; 16:13). Who but God could do such mighty works as these?

The Spirit is the Counsellor, or *paraclete* (John 14:16; 15:26; 16:7). *Paraclete* comes from the Greek *para*, 'beside,' and *kaleo*, 'to call'. It signifies that the Spirit is called to our side for the purpose of giving us whatever help is necessary in our Christian lives.

THE GIFTS OF THE SPIRIT

In Romans 12:6–8, 1 Corinthians 12:8–10 and Ephesians 4:11 Paul gives us lists of spiritual gifts. But are these gifts of the Spirit intended for the apostolic period of the first century only, or should they be manifested within the life of the church today? Is what some Christians claim to be the work of the Spirit nothing more than psychologically induced reactions to certain kinds of stimuli? Could it be the work of Satan? This was the charge that the Pharisees made against Jesus (Matthew 12:24). We need to recognize that which comes from God, that which comes from Satan and that which comes from our natural selves. Everything must be tested by the Spirit of Scripture.

In 1 Corinthians 13 we read, '... *where there are prophecies, they will cease; where there are tongues, they will be stilled; where there is knowledge, it will pass away*' (v. 8). This will occur '*when perfection comes*' (v. 10). But when is this time of perfection? Has it already happened, or is it yet to be expected? Have the gifts ceased or not?

Many Christians believe that certain gifts of the Spirit, such as healings, miracles, and tongues, are no longer relevant. They would, however, accept that the Spirit still gives to his people gifts that are vital to the ministry of the church. These would include gifts such as the ability to lead or teach. On the other hand, members of the so-called Charismatic Movement believe that all of the *charismata* or supernatural gifts of the Spirit are to continue until Jesus comes again.

The Greek word *charisma* (plural, *charismata*), from which our English word *charismatic* is derived, refers to gifts God has given by his Spirit to Christians. At its root is the word *charis*, which means grace. So it follows that the gifts of the Spirit are not an award for exceptional zeal or accomplishment. A gift is, by definition, something freely given. And so we can't take credit for this; it is a gift from God.

When we study the word *charisma* in the New Testament, it becomes clear that it is not confined to gifts such as healing or speaking in tongues. It applies to whatever gifts the Spirit uses for working in our lives, and in the life of the church. Since God has given all Christians at least one spiritual gift, the entire church of Jesus Christ is charismatic. It is, therefore, somewhat misleading to call Pentecostalism or Neo-Pentecostalism the Charismatic Movement.

I find it difficult to see how any of the gifts of the Spirit can be limited to one brief period as many Christians suggest. If they are, then it appears that a substantial section of 1 Corinthians is only a recollection of things which are now long since passed. For instance, chapter 14 serves a limited purpose, other than historical interest, if the gift of tongues has now become obsolete in the life of the church. Furthermore, there is no clear statement in Scripture that the gifts are not for the people of Christ in any generation. Quite the contrary! '... *this is what was spoken by the prophet Joel: "In the last days, God says, I will pour out my Spirit on all people." ...'* The gift to which Joel primarily pointed was prophecy. However, 'the last days' and 'all people' surely suggest that the signs and wonders are not restricted to one brief period (Acts 2:16–21; see Joel 2:28–32).

It is important, however, to qualify what I have said. I believe that not all of what is practised in churches today is from God. It may be the result of deception, the result of someone's imagination, or the result of an evil spirit of divination. People claiming to be gifted by the Spirit are known to have divided churches and caused great damage. I also believe that the continuance of the gifts of the Spirit is not necessarily to say that this applies to every generation. The sovereignty of the Spirit means that he gives his gifts to whom he pleases, when he pleases; that is his prerogative. As a result, he has been more active in some periods than in others.

PROPHECY

The prophet's message often, but not always, concerned the future. Hence, Old Testament prophets were sometimes described as 'seers' because they saw things as God saw them and what was going to happen as a result. A prophet's concern with the future was usually influenced by the behaviour of God's people in the present. That is, the prophet revealed what would happen if the people did not repent. The prophets never revealed the future for the sake of the future; rather, it was to address the present.

The Bible repeatedly warns us against people who claim to be prophets when really they are not. We are told about false prophets such as Zedekiah (1 Kings 22) and Hananiah (Jeremiah 28). '*... many false prophets will appear and deceive many* *people'* (Matthew 24:11). They will often pose as Christians but teach things that oppose God's Word. Although it may not be the conscious aim of these prophets to cause chaos, their influence will inevitably be destructive. Therefore, we need to be like the Bereans, who examined the Scriptures every day to see if what Paul said was true (Acts 17:11). Most cults begin by its leader or leaders claiming to have access to new revelation from God.

Is prophecy a continuing gift within the church? Certainly the Bible is complete and must not be added to in any way. But that is not to say there are no instances in which God appears to have given insight to an individual. The story of the nineteenth-century preacher C.H. Spurgeon while preaching at the Surrey Gardens Music Hall is a good example of this. He suddenly pointed to a man in the crowd and said, 'There is a man sitting there, who is a shoemaker; he keeps his shop open on Sundays, it was open last Sabbath morning, he took ninepence, and there was fourpence profit out of it; his soul is sold to Satan for fourpence!'[1] All that Spurgeon said turned out to be true and was the means by which the man was led to conversion. Spurgeon continues to say that he could tell of other cases in which similar things happened. Numerous predictions such as this could be quoted from Christian history.

Paul in 1 Corinthians 12:8–10 writes, *'To one there is given ... the message of wisdom, to another the message of knowledge by means of the same Spirit ... to another prophecy ...'* There are people who say that there is little, if any, difference between these three gifts. But they are, I believe, clearly distinguishable. The Greek word we have translated as *wisdom* is *Sophia*. It is wisdom which knows God, while knowledge – the Greek word is *gnosis* – has to do with the practical application of wisdom to life's situations. Though the popular understanding of prophecy is foretelling things which will occur, it more often means telling forth the Word of God. Thus, every preacher and teacher anointed by the Spirit may be called a prophet.

Some Christians who oppose prophecy as a continuing gift within the church react in a different way towards preaching. But surely if the sufficiency of Scripture is interpreted in such an inflexible way that their reaction to the suggestion of prophecy indicates, a preacher should do nothing but read the Scriptures. Any preaching would be additional to the actual words of Scripture.

God, I believe, still speaks through people today. I also believe that there are different levels of prophecy. There are prophecies recorded in the Bible which are applicable to every generation. In contrast there are prophets whose words are only applicable for those to whom they speak. They convey a special message from God regarding how he views a person or situation, and maybe what is going to happen.

Paul in 1 Thessalonians 5:19–21 says, 'Do not put out the Spirit's fire; do not treat prophecies with contempt. Test everything. …' Here we have a double warning. First, it is necessary to listen when the Spirit speaks. At the same time it would be a serious error to believe that every utterance is from the Spirit. Maybe it is just the person who speaks, or even demonic power using human lips. That is why in 1 Corinthians 12:10 we see that the gift of prophecy is immediately followed by the gift of discernment. A gift that would be redundant, if there is no such gift as prophecy today.

The test of true prophets is the truthfulness of their prophecies (Deuteronomy 18:21,22). Non-fulfilment of a prophecy is proof that it is false, but the fulfilment of prophecy is not a guarantee of its genuineness. Moses reminded the Israelites of a false prophet's prediction being fulfilled (Deuteronomy 13:1–4). How, then, can we discern the false from the true? The answer is that true prophets of God will minister in complete harmony with all that Scripture says. Hence, our safeguard against falsehood and false prophets is to know the truth. To spot a counterfeit, we need to be familiar with the real thing.

TONGUES

The first clear reference to the biblical phenomenon of speaking in tongues, or *glossolalia* as it is commonly called, happened on the day of Pentecost in the city of Jerusalem (Acts 2:1–13). The believers were all together in one place when suddenly the most important event recorded in Acts occurred. *'All of them were filled with the Holy Spirit and began to speak in other tongues as the Spirit enabled them'* (v. 4). This strange phenomenon attracted a crowd who were bewildered because *'each one heard them speaking in his own language'* (v. 6). So the crowd asks, *'Then how is it that each of us hears them in his own native language?'* (v. 8); and they continue, *'… we hear them declaring the wonders of God in our own tongues!'* (v. 11). Here a miracle took place in that the speakers used languages not previously known by them, but perfectly understood by the hearers.

Some people assert that this miracle relates more to the hearers than to the speakers. That is, the people heard in the different languages, while the believers only spoke in their own language. However, such a belief is unsupportable for several reasons. Not least there is the statement that those who were filled with the Holy Spirit spoke in different tongues.

What was the purpose of speaking in these other languages? Why was such a miracle necessary? We do not read that people were converted by hearing their different languages spoken. Furthermore, when Peter preaches to the crowd in one language, probably his native Aramaic, everyone understands him. Nor is there any evidence that these Spirit-filled believers continued speaking these different languages in their subsequent missionary work. Thus it would appear that their utterances were of an ecstatic nature, glorifying God for the great things he had done.

The book of Acts contains two other clear examples of this gift. First, Cornelius and his household spoke with tongues and praised God when they believed the gospel message of Peter (Acts 10:44–48). Secondly, when Paul laid his hands on a group of disciples the Holy Spirit came, evidencing his presence by enabling them to speak in other tongues and to prophesy (Acts 19:1–7).

A detailed role of tongues in the church is to be found in 1 Corinthians 14. Here there are some differences to the account in Acts. In the Corinthian church, ecstatic speech has to be interpreted, whereas at Pentecost the hearers do not need interpreters because they hear their own languages. In addition, we observe that in Acts a message is brought to outsiders, but in 1 Corinthians it is primarily for private worship directed to God (14:2,4,19). Speaking to him in tongues is comparable to personal prayer. Whether we consider this speech to be a known language or an ecstatic utterance of sounds which seem to be of no known language does not alter Paul's guidance to the church.

Paul, in his comparison of tongues and prophecy, emphasizes that the latter is far superior because it is of real help to the whole church. He accepts tongues as a genuine gift from personal experience (v. 18). But if it is a gift that is used in public it needs to be interpreted. If there is no interpreter, the speaker must remain

17

silent. Everyone present needs to understand what is happening. Thus Paul reaches the logical conclusion that it is better to speak five understandable words that will help others than ten thousand unintelligible sounds.

The gift of tongues appears to have been popular in the Corinthian church and maybe elsewhere, even though Paul does not directly refer to tongues in his other letters. It was a supernatural and highly desired gift. But it was creating serious problems in the worship services. This church was blessed with spiritual gifts (1 Corinthians 1:5–7), but misunderstood their proper usage (12:1), especially that of the gift of tongues. Their self-centered ambition and a desire to hear themselves speak, rather than to edify the church, resulted in meaningless utterances and chaos. Despite this, Paul does not denigrate the gift of tongues. He says, '... *do not forbid speaking in tongues. But everything should be done in a fitting and orderly way*' (1 Corinthians 14:39,40).

In Acts 10 we see that as Peter was speaking, the Holy Spirit came upon the hearers: *The circumcised believers who had come with Peter were astonished that the gift of the Holy Spirit had been poured out even on the Gentiles. For they heard them speaking in tongues and praising God*' (vv.45,46). Verse 46 leaves us in no doubt that the outward form of this outpouring of the Holy Spirit resulted in them speaking in tongues.

The ability to speak in tongues, however, is not necessarily a sign of the presence of the Holy Spirit. There are, I believe, four possible explanations. Tongues may be divinely, satanically, psychologically, or artificially produced. The latter three are dangerous. They can cause irreconcilable differences within a fellowship that may lead to a tragic split.

There needs to be in worship a balance between thought and

feeling. Maintaining sound doctrine is vital. At the same time we need to express our emotions and gratitude to God. We must not become slaves to orders of service. Surely, a realization of what God has done in Jesus Christ to save us not only challenges us, but should result in a sense of awe, of orderliness, of thankfulness, and of exuberant joy.

THE FULLNESS OF THE SPIRIT

The church today needs, more than anything else, to be filled with the Spirit of God. Any Christian who is not filled with the Holy Spirit is defective. Being continuously filled with the Spirit is never an optional extra, it is a necessity. Ephesians 5:18 is an apostolic injunction which is significant for believers today. *'Do not get drunk on wine, which leads to debauchery. Instead, be filled with the Spirit.'* Here we have a contrast between a drunkard who is controlled by alcohol and a Christian whose life is to be under the control of the Spirit. To be filled with the Spirit is the most important commandment in the Bible. Because if we obey this commandment, we spontaneously obey all the others.

The meaning of the word 'filled', as Paul used it, is not a picture of a container into which something is placed until it is full. Rather, it is to be permeated by the Holy Spirit's influence. As the fragrance of Mary's ointment filled the house (John 12:3); the influence of the Spirit should utterly control the believer's life.

The question every Christian must ask is, 'Why do I want to be filled with the Spirit?' Is it to glorify God or myself? An example of the latter is found in Acts 8. Simon the sorcerer *'believed and was baptised. And he followed Philip everywhere, astonished by the great signs and miracles he saw'* (v. 13). *'When Simon saw that the Spirit was given at the laying on of the apostles' hands, he offered them money and said, "Give me also this ability so that everyone on whom I lay my hands may receive the Holy Spirit"* (vv. 18,19). Here, he thought, was an opportunity to possess great power and prestige. Peter's answer was swift and severe. He tells him that he can have no part in this ministry, because his heart is not right before God (v. 21). Simon fails to see that the Spirit's power is to glorify God alone.

What does it mean to be baptized by the Spirit? When is a believer baptized by the Spirit? Is there a second baptism? These are questions upon which Christians disagree.

Some Christians believe that there is no clear biblical support for a separate post-conversion baptism of the Spirit. They believe that the baptism of the Spirit referred to in the Bible is when the Spirit comes to dwell within the believer at the time of conversion (1 Corinthians 12:13). Hence, if you are a Christian, the Spirit of God lives in you; if you are not a Christian, you do not have the Spirit. Why then, they would argue, does a Christian need a second baptism when the Spirit is already present? Peter Masters, in his book, *Only One Baptism of the Holy Spirit*[2] supports this view.

Other Christians talk of a 'second baptism' or a 'second blessing' of the Spirit following conversion. There are many who, some time after they are born again, experience God meeting with them in a new and powerful way. In charismatic circles this is commonly known as the baptism in the Spirit. Some 'traditional' evangelicals would agree that there is another baptism to be experienced after conversion. Those who have read Martyn Lloyd-Jones' book *Joy Unspeakable* and his sermons on Ephesians 1 published by the Banner of Truth Trust will know that he believed that you can be a true believer, and still not have received the baptism of the Holy Spirit.

David Watson, who I knew from the time he was curate-in-charge of St Cuthbert's, York in the 1960s, spoke of how he had experienced the Holy Spirit in a new and powerful way subsequent to his conversion. Later he visited Lloyd-Jones in Westminster. Lloyd-Jones listened and then said, 'You've been baptized with the Holy Spirit.'

David Watson considered what had been said and came to a different conclusion. He believed, with great respect, that Lloyd-Jones was mistaken. He in no way doubted the reality of the experience, but he did doubt the biblical terminology. David believed that the biblical description was not 'baptism in the Spirit' – that, he considered to be the initiatory work whereby Christ baptizes us in the Spirit into his body. The biblical terminology, David claimed, was 'filled with the Spirit'.

The infilling of the Spirit's power to serve is a recurring feature within the New Testament. Again and again Christians were empowered to serve. Take for instance the book of Acts (2:4; 4:8,31: 9:17; 13:9). Some of those who had previously been blessed at Pentecost received further outpourings so that they could boldly face some new challenge. The purpose of the infilling of the Spirit is always power for service.

It is interesting to note that these fillings of the Spirit are usually referred to in terms of a practical result, and not in terms of how they felt. I am always wary of people who speak exclusively about the Spirit. That is because he never draws attention to himself, but to Christ. Jesus said, *'He will bring glory to me by taking from what is mine and making it known to you'* (John 16:14). No one in the Bible said, 'I am filled with the Spirit.' Rather, it was recognized by others. And there is no mention of wild, ecstatic behaviour. Instead, the only feelings associated with the Spirit are those of joy and love.

How are we to obtain the Spirit's power so as to glorify God?

The answer is that we should pray specifically and persistently for it. Jesus said to his disciples, *'If you then, though you are evil, know how to give good gifts to your children, how much more will your Father in heaven give the Holy Spirit to those who ask him!'* (Luke 11:13). This assures us that our prayers to our Father in heaven will be heard. God imparted the power of the Holy Spirit at Pentecost. He still does to those who seek him (Acts 4:31) and obey him (Acts 5:32).

THE FRUIT OF THE SPIRIT

What is the 'fruit' of the Spirit? What should we expect to see in a person who has received the Spirit as promised by Jesus? Paul provides the answer: '... *the fruit of the Spirit is love, joy, peace, patience, kindness, goodness, faithfulness, gentleness and self-control. Against such things there is no law'* (Galatians 5:22,23) Paul is not here referring to the special individual gifts specified in 1 Corinthians 12, but rather to characteristics that should all be manifest in the life of every Christian.

Mentioned at the beginning of the above list of Christian virtues is the greatest of all – namely, love. A love of God and then others dictates how we behave. It is no exaggeration to say that love is the mother of all Christian virtues. Having said that, we need to realize that there are several different Greek words translated 'love' in English. For instance, in the New Testament the Greek word *agape* is often used to describe God's love for his Son, for us, and also for how we are to love others. When Jesus said, 'Love your enemies', Matthew uses the word *agape* (Matthew 5:44). When 1 John 4:16 says, *'God is love'*, it uses the word *agape*. That is the kind of love that God has. In the same verse we are told to love as God does. This *agape* love is evidence that the Holy Spirit is at work within our lives.

More often than not, people see love only as a feeling or desire.

But *agape* love is much more. It is a love that eagerly seeks the opportunity to do something good to help someone else, even to death (John 15:13). God's ultimate expression of his love was when he sent his Son to die for our sins.

True *agape* love is a love which involves action. We see this well illustrated in the story told by Jesus of the good Samaritan (see Luke 10:25–37). A Jew travelling from Jerusalem to Jericho was attacked by robbers. They stripped him of his possessions, beat him up, and left him half dead. Would anyone come to his aid? A Jewish priest saw him lying there but passed by. He did not want to get involved. A Levite saw the injured man, but he also passed by. Finally there came a Samaritan and, despite there being great hostility between the Jews and the Samaritans, he showed practical love to a person in desperate need. That is how Jesus defines love. It is *agape* love, the fruit of the Spirit.

What must we do to ensure that we bear the fruit of the Spirit in our lives? Again, Paul provides the answer. He tells us that 'Those who belong to Christ Jesus have crucified the sinful nature with its passions and desires. Since we live by the Spirit, let us keep in step with the Spirit' (Galatians 5:24,25).

As we crucify our sinful nature by repudiating what we know to be wrong, so too we must walk by the Spirit, thus doing what we know to be right. Yielding passively to the Spirit's control is not enough; it is also necessary to walk actively in the Spirit's way. Is there any sin in our lives which prevents this? Is there an unsuitable relationship with another person that needs to be changed? Whatever the cause may be, it must be brought to Christ in confession and repentance. Only then can we see the fruit of the Spirit in our lives. This, along with the gifts of the Spirit, is essential both to the health of the Christian and of the church.

NOTES

1. *C.H. Spurgeon: The Early Years: Volume 1* compiled by Susannah Spurgeon and Joseph Harrald (Edinburgh: Banner of Truth Trust, 1967) pp. 531–2.

2. Peter Masters, *Only One Baptism of the Holy Spirit* (London: The Wakeman Trust, 1994).

CHAPTER 2

MIRACLES

A mother collected her son from Sunday school and asked what Bible story they had studied.

'It was about Jericho,' he replied.

'So what happened?' asked the mother.

He told her of how Joshua and his army had fired nuclear rockets at the city walls. Then, when the walls collapsed, the army entered with their guns and shot all the inhabitants.

Mother, in a state of disbelief said, 'I'm sure you didn't learn that.'

'No,' replied her son. 'But if I told you what did happen, you'd never believe it!'

A story similar to that is sometimes quoted by preachers to introduce an out of the ordinary and exceptional event such as the collapse of the walls of formidable Jericho (Joshua 6:1–20). Joshua told the Israelites, *'When you hear ... the trumpets ... give a loud shout; then the wall of the city will collapse and ... [you will go] straight in'* (v. 5). How can anyone reasonably try to explain this? A shout, no matter how loud, is unlikely to bring down the solid walls of a city. Are we embarrassed by assuming that no one could be expected to take such a fantastic story seriously? Do we ignore it, trivialize it, or seek a natural explanation? Perhaps we say, 'I can't believe impossible things.' Alternatively we may accept that certain stories spread throughout the Bible clearly testify to the direct intervention of an all-powerful Creator God. Do miracles really happen, or are they a figment of the imagination? Let us begin by asking ourselves some pertinent questions.

WHAT IS A MIRACLE?

The word 'miracle' is used in several different ways. We have probably heard comments such as, 'It's a miracle no one was seriously injured in that accident,' or 'It's a miracle he passed his exams.' This particular usage refers to the occurrence of an extremely unexpected or unlikely event. In contrast, the miracles referred to in the Bible are much more than what is improbable; they are definite divine actions.

Is it a miracle when we pray for God to provide a material need and then receive exactly what was required? Is it a miracle if we unexpectedly meet someone at the exact moment we need to? These and many similar events, although often called miracles, are not what Scripture classifies as such. Rather, they are acts of providence, maybe as answers to prayer, of how God orchestrates our daily lives.

Dictionaries sometimes define miracles as events that violate at least one accepted law of nature. Such a definition is, I believe, inadequate for how can we justify the idea of a God who violates the very laws he used to create and run his universe. To talk of laws suggests the presence of a lawgiver, and if laws are set up

26

by an omnipotent God, it surely follows that they could also be changed or temporarily halted according to his good pleasure. To argue that because things normally happen in a certain way, they can only ever happen in that way, would be irrational.

The laws of nature as defined by today's scientists are in many ways different to those suggested by their predecessors. Our scientific understanding of the universe is still incomplete, and so revisions and rejections occur as our understanding of the universe increases. Consequently, we should not presumptuously reject miracles because they are not corroborated by our present knowledge of the laws of nature.

For a person who believes in God, it is better to say that a miracle can very simply be defined as a natural event behaving in an unnatural way because of a supernatural cause. Hence, a miracle cannot adequately be explained by any natural means. Let us take, as an example, the story of Moses and the burning bush (Exodus 3:1–3). Moses saw that though the bush was on fire it did not burn up. This was a natural event in that it was an ordinary bush. It was an unnatural event in that the fire, the form in which the angel of the Lord appeared, did not consume the bush. And the reason why the bush did not end up a pile of ashes was because the fire had a supernatural cause. No natural explanation will suffice for this event. Likewise, Jesus, while at a wedding celebration, changed water into wine of the highest quality (John 2:1–11). This was natural water. It was an unnatural event in that water does not normally turn to wine. The reason it did so was because of a supernatural cause. The Bible tells us that God made it happen. This simple pattern of natural, unnatural and supernatural events is applicable to all miracles.

Obviously, from what as been said, it is impossible to observe a complete miracle. We might see the result, but certainly not the cause. For that reason, miracles cannot be explained or explored by repeated scientific observation and experiment. This is not a criticism of science, but it reveals that science has limitations. Does science contradict Scripture? The answer is no. Scripture and science, properly interpreted, do not conflict, but rather they address different issues. Scripture tells us who created the world (Genesis 1:1) and why (Isaiah 43:7). Science, on the other hand, is concerned with the systematic observation of and experimentation with phenomena relating to the physical universe. Although the scientific method is extremely valuable for studying natural phenomena, it cannot ever legitimately explain, one way or the other, the supernatural. Miracles by their very nature are unpredictable events that cannot be replicated in a laboratory.

It is not unreasonable to assume that most people, if they saw a miracle occur, would have doubts about whether it actually took place. Suppose someone told you about a glass of water that turned to wine and then back to water. How would you react? Probably your first reaction would be to seek a logical explanation. Had the person imagined it? Was it a trick? Are you convinced by the trustworthiness of the person who bears witness to this event?

Now let us take this supposition a stage further and assume that there is a reliable witness who clearly saw what happened. Again, how would you react? Could this person perhaps have momentarily hallucinated or have made an error of judgment? Finally, we are told that a security video camera had been present and recorded the whole event. One frame shows water, the next wine, followed by water. Is this incontrovertible evidence that a miracle occurred? Instead, is it possible that the security tape had been tampered with? Or maybe it was trick photography? Usually, whatever the strength of evidence to support a miracle, people will seek a logical explanation for something that is illogical to their understanding. As a consequence, doubts will inevitably arise. Seeing miraculous signs does not necessarily convince people of the truth. Jesus knew that however many miracles some people saw, they still would not believe (John 12:37)!

DO MIRACLES HAVE NATURAL EXPLANATIONS?

Numerous natural causes are suggested to doubt or deny the occurrence of miracles. Surely, it is claimed, there are perfectly rational or scientific explanations for all such unusual events. As an example, let us again consider the phenomenon of the burning bush. Not surprisingly, this has been widely discussed because of its observable uniqueness. Was this a manifestation of God himself? Or is it possible to provide a natural explanation?

There are those who tell us that the strong sunlight shining upon coloured leaves, berries or crimson flowers produced an illusion of a bush engulfed in flames. Another suggestion is a perennial herb called *Dictamnus albus*. This plant is known to produce an inflammable, volatile oil that can be ignited by a naked light. For this reason it is commonly called the burning bush. Despite momentarily bursting into flame, the plant remains uninjured. Could this, or a plant with similar characteristics, be the answer? Some Bible commentators consider this experience of Moses' to be visionary or even a figment of his imagination. This, however, is pure conjecture, for nowhere are we told that this was imaginary or a vision. Indeed whatever suggestions are used to explain this unique experience, they cannot satisfactorily contradict the biblical text. That is, Moses saw a bush; it was on fire, but did not burn. Unquestionably the event is unusual, for

Moses – a man who had many years experience of observing all forms of desert life – was amazed and decided to take a closer look at this very strange phenomenon.

How did Jesus turn water in six large stone jars into wine? Is there a possible natural explanation for this abnormal transformation? A popular suggestion is that these jars had recently been filled with wine and that the remaining sediment when mixed with the water explains what happened. Although this theory is imaginative, it is unlikely. Would such dilute wine be praised as the finest of the feast (John 2:10)? As has often been said, many of the suggested natural explanations are more difficult to believe than the miracles themselves. Even so, they may be preferred to the admission of a miracle.

There are two wrong attitudes that people commonly adopt towards miracles. One attitude is to exaggerate them and so make miracles more spectacular than they are. The other extreme is to always try to discount God's activity by attempting to find a natural explanation for any unnatural occurrence. These two opposing attitudes can be well illustrated by taking as an example the miracle of the coin in the fish's mouth.

Jesus said to Peter, '... *go to the lake and throw out your line. Take the first fish you catch; open its mouth and you will find a four-drachma coin. Take it and give it to them for my tax and yours*' (Matthew 17:27). That is exactly what happened. In spite of that, there are people who try to find a natural explanation for this supernatural event. Some will dismiss it as fable; others think that Peter caught a fish and sold it, then with the proceeds paid the Temple tax for Jesus and himself. This explanation, however, does not in any way account for the fact that Matthew states that the coin would be found within the mouth of the fish.

At the other extreme are those who exaggerate this miracle

into something that it never was. How then might we reasonably explain what happened? It is a known fact that some species of fish regularly pick up small objects such as brightly coloured pebbles, bottle tops or coins. Therefore, it is not unreasonable to assume that that is how this fish came to have a coin in its mouth. God provided a fish to pick up the right coin, at the right time, and then swim with it in a certain direction.

Peter tried to retrieve something from the water, and the Bible tells us that God enabled him to do so at his first attempt. Natural explanations as to how this was achieved need not necessarily discount God's activity, for the miracle is, more often than not, that he made it happen just at the right moment. The Red Sea parted because of a strong east wind so that the Israelites could pass through on dry land at the exact time they needed to (Exodus 14:21,22). In contrast, the Egyptians who followed the Israelites were drowned – 'Not one of them survived' (v. 28). The Lord thus used natural means in punishing evil and also in guiding and protecting his people.

It is often said that the incident of Jonah being swallowed by a great fish is based upon fiction rather than fact. Rationalistic unbelief would argue that such an amazing story cannot be accepted as literally true. Surely no sane person could take such a bizarre story seriously! Certainly it must be the most discussed fish that ever swam in the Mediterranean. How can Jonah remain inside a fish for three days and three nights and then be spat out alive on a beach? I suggest that the miracle is not whether this could or could not happen, but rather that it happened at exactly the right place, on the right day, at the right moment to save him from drowning. This was no accident. '... the LORD provided a great fish to swallow Jonah' (Jonah 1:17). Be that as it may, I have actually heard people attempt to deny God's activity by speculating that Jonah swam ashore and spent three nights in an inn called 'The Fish'!

Of course, it is theoretically possible that all the above successes were due to chance. Therefore, is it possible to ascertain how unlikely something actually is? Are the odds for the above events occurring statistically so overwhelmingly improbable that the intervention of a supernatural power provides a more likely explanation?

People in the ancient world were much more willing to believe that God or lesser supernatural beings were active in nature. As a result, natural phenomena such as thunder, lightning, earthquakes, floods and rainbows were regarded as direct divine action. Today we are aware that there are natural explanations for these and many other suchlike phenomena. Despite this there are many biblical accounts which, if true, must be due to a supernatural cause. The overwhelming evidence that Jesus was raised from the dead and left the tomb is a good example of a situation that cannot be satisfactorily explained by human reasoning. Regardless of this, there are some non-Christians who will attempt to explain the bodily resurrection by natural causes.

The so-called 'swoon' theory, whereby Jesus only fainted and was then revived in the cool of the tomb, has many supporters. Does not the fact that Jesus 'died' much sooner than most victims of crucifixion support this theory? The answer is very simple. Any natural explanation denies the testimony of the biblical authors and numerous eyewitnesses. Paul writes about some of these appearances: '... *he appeared to Peter, and then to the Twelve. After that, he appeared to more than five hundred of the brothers at the same time ... Then he appeared to James, then to all the apostles, and last of all he appeared to me also ...*' (1 Corinthians 15:5–8).

Alternatively, some early opponents of Christianity suggested that the followers of Jesus stole his body from the tomb and then proclaimed the story of the resurrection (Matthew 28:11–15). Or maybe someone else removed the body without the Christians knowing about it. This was the initial reaction of Mary Magdalene when she discovered that the tomb was empty (John 20:2). These and other natural explanations, which deny the death and resurrection of Christ, are not corroborated by the overwhelming evidence. For example, prior to the resurrection the disciples were afraid and without hope. But after the resurrection they fearlessly praised God. Saul of Tarsus, who later became known as Paul, was an enemy of Christianity until the risen Christ spoke to him. Anyone who understands human nature knows people do not change that much without some major influence.

The foremost test of any miracle is not to consider its theoretical possibility or impossibility. Rather it is to ascertain whether or not the witnesses are reliable. If a testimony is sound, we are obliged to consider it seriously and without prejudice. But there are some people who, whatever the evidence or number of witnesses, will not be convinced by the miracle accounts. A primary reason for this is that the mid seventeenth century saw the development of a philosophy called Deism. A deist believes in a personal God who created the universe, but later withdrew and no longer controls it. This suggests that God created the universe like a clock which he wound up and then left to run automatically without him ever intervening again. Because deists believe that everything is governed by the steadfast laws of nature, it follows that miracles are impossible. A non-interventionist God would not change the mechanism he once made. This way of thinking, popularized by the eighteenth-century Scottish philosopher David Hume, goes some way towards explaining how Western society began to reject its belief in miracles. Hume was so sceptical about miracles that he assumed the only genuine one was that people could believe in any of them.

There are people who go a stage further and claim not to be deists but atheists; they believe that God does not exist and that our universe evolved by chance. Then there are the agnostics; people who believe that no one can know whether God exists, or indeed that anything exists which cannot be empirically investigated. In sharp contrast, a sincere believer of the Bible relies not on research but on revelation, and will accept that God is God Almighty, Creator of the heavens and the earth – and still controls them. For this reason, miracles are possible and, furthermore, probable.

I'VE NEVER SEEN A MIRACLE

It is very easy to skim through parts of the Bible and receive the impression that miracles were a common occurrence. That would be a serious mistake. A fact that we must come to terms with is that miracles were an extremely rare occurrence even in biblical times. For the most part, they were associated with specific, relatively brief periods such as the period of Moses and Joshua, during the ministries of Elijah and Elisha, and in the time of Jesus and the early disciples. Miracles did occur at other periods in the Bible, but were much less frequent. In the time of Isaiah, for example, divine intervention defeated Sennacherib's large army (2 Kings 19:35,36). In the time of Daniel, God preserved Shadrach, Meshach and Abednego in the fiery furnace (Daniel 3:19–28). These supernatural events, however, were not the usual way in which God dealt with his people.

Miracles by definition are contrary to the natural course of events, and so are rare. A miracle would not be a miracle if it was a common event. Thus the vast majority of people will never have personally witnessed one. But is this a valid reason to doubt their existence? Certainly not. I have never experienced a tsunami, yet it would be foolish of me, considering the reliable evidence of other people, to reject such an occurrence. Likewise with a miracle, it is necessary to consider the trustworthiness and evidence of those who claim to have experienced one, and not discount the possibility because we cannot verify the facts ourselves.

It is sometimes said, 'If God would perform a miracle, sign or wonder, I would believe!' But when we read the Bible we see that this is not necessarily so. God brought the Israelites out of bondage in Egypt and yet, despite witnessing many spectacular miracles, they repeatedly experienced periods of apostasy and failure. In Exodus 15, following their miraculous crossing of the Red Sea and the destruction of the Egyptian armies, the Israelites exalted their God with songs and praises. In contrast, only three days later, they grumbled against Moses for bringing them into a wilderness where they could find no water fit to drink. Their grumbling ultimately represented dissatisfaction with God, who was responsible for appointing Moses.

All sorts of people witnessed the miracles of Jesus. Healing was a common feature of his earthly ministry, as we shall see in the next chapter. Even so, irrespective of all that he did, Jesus was repeatedly rejected and ridiculed. Today there are many people throughout the world who, like the inquisitive Herod Antipas, would like to see the performance of some sign or miracle (Luke 23:8). And, if they did, how would they react? History reveals that people have the apparent freedom to shut their eyes and ears to the truth. Clearly, faith in God is not based upon physical senses but on the inner conviction of the Holy Spirit. That is why the miracle accounts frequently reveal that while some people believed, others did not.

Why does God perform miracles? Are they mere arbitrary demonstrations of his power? No, they are not. Nor does God perform miracles simply to overwhelm people with wonder or to satisfy their curiosity. Jesus refused to perform a miraculous sign to prove himself or substantiate his claims (Matthew 12:38ff.). Why was Jesus not prepared to give them visual proof? The reason is that it was unnecessary, for he had already provided all the requisite evidence. We should never seek a miraculous sign to substantiate the sufficiency of Scripture. God himself declares that his word is sufficient (Psalm 19:7; 2 Timothy 3:15–17). The Bible is an adequate and accurate record of our need to believe in God's greatest miracle – the new birth that he has promised to all who believe in the Lord Jesus Christ.

Miracles are signs that point to something or someone. In 1 Kings 17, Elijah revealed the almighty power and abounding love of his God by reviving a widow's dead son. He brought the child down from the upstairs room, gave him to his mother, and said, '*Look, your son is alive!*' (v. 23). And how did the widow respond? The woman told Elijah, 'Now I know that you are a man of God and that the word of the LORD from your mouth is the truth' (v. 24).

In John 10, Jesus was surrounded by the Jewish leaders. They asked, '*"How long will you keep us in suspense? If you are the Christ, tell us plainly." Jesus answered, "I did tell you, but you do not believe. The miracles I do in my Father's name speak for me"*' (10:24,25). On the day of Pentecost, Peter told the crowd that God publicly endorsed Jesus of Nazareth by doing miracles, wonders and signs through him, as they well knew (Acts 2:22). Furthermore, we are told that the apostles also '*performed many miraculous signs and wonders among the people*' (Acts 5:12; see also 2:43;). This was the result of the Spirit's power, and thus pointed to the authenticity of divinely commissioned teachers and leaders. Therefore it follows that true miracles will point to the redemptive purpose of God and must agree with all that Scripture says.

ARE ALL MIRACLES, SIGNS AND WONDERS FROM GOD?

It is important to be aware that not all manifestations of supernatural power are proof of divine intervention. Neither are they proof that the human agent is divinely commissioned. Pagan priests, witchdoctors, magicians and others are known to have performed miraculous feats under the influence of demonic power. The Bible warns Christians to be wary of false signs and miracles – very believable ones – which are aimed at leading people away from the truth. These will be the major tool of Satan in the last days.

The teaching of Jesus was that on Judgment Day many would say to him: *'"Lord, Lord, did we not prophesy in your name, and in your name drive out demons and perform many miracles?" Then I will tell them plainly, "I never knew you. Away from me, you evildoers!"'* (Matthew 7:22,23).

These people may believe that they are doing the work of the Lord but obviously, since he calls them evildoers, they are not. They are deceived and have been used by Satan to deceive others. They cannot, however, fool Jesus, the Judge and Lord before whom they must finally appear.

God, at times, allows Satan to exert influence upon the physical realm. For instance, we know that God gave Satan permission to attack Job, but the power granted him was evidently limited (Job 1:12; 2:6). Satan does nothing without the permission of God. The confrontation between the prophets of Baal and Elijah on Mount Carmel is a good example of this. Satan, despite being able to perform great and miraculous signs, could not send down fire from heaven. Why was that? The answer is that in this instance, God would not permit it because it was a direct challenge between himself and Baal as to who was the true God (1 Kings 18:24).

There are some things that are beyond our control, but we need not worry, for although Satan may win some battles, he cannot win the war. Those who have put their trust in Jesus are certainly on the winning side. This is because Satan is a creature, and thus has limited power, while God is omnipotent and does exactly what he pleases with his creation (Psalm 135:6).

DO MIRACLES STILL HAPPEN TODAY?

God is the same God and the universe and humankind have not altered in decisive ways since the time of creation. For this reason I suggest that a miracle is no less likely to happen today than it did in the past, unless it can be proved that God no longer does such things. That, however, would contradict numerous personal statements of apparently reliable witnesses to the miraculous in every generation since biblical times. Could it be that all these people were deluded? Maybe what happened were always mere coincidences or natural anomalies. Or is it more likely that God still interacts with his creation so that it does what he wants it to do?

I am of the opinion that many unusual events today are misinterpreted as miracles. There are some people who have an insatiable appetite for the paranormal and make claims that are bizarre to the point of stupidity. Their claims have nothing in common with Scripture. I do, however, believe that God still intervenes supernaturally in nature and human affairs when he has a good reason to do so. Moreover, I believe that God can, and sometimes will, heal people apart from conventional methods, and this will be considered in the next chapter. I believe that what is impossible from a human perspective is possible for an all-powerful Creator God who made the universe and all that is in it.

CHAPTER 3

MIRACULOUS HEALING

The Bible tells us that God heals the sick. Probably the most familiar Old Testament example in relation to this is the miraculous healing of Naaman, who had leprosy (2 Kings 5:1–14). Naaman washed himself seven times in the River Jordan, as instructed by Elisha, the prophet of God, and his flesh became healthy. Infinitely more importantly than that, a spiritual miracle accompanied the physical one; his soul was healed as well as his body. This is evident from his subsequent conduct.

In the New Testament, we repeatedly read about Jesus and his followers healing people. Jesus appears to have healed people almost everywhere he went, by word or touch. Sight was restored to the blind and hearing to the deaf, the lame were able to walk, those with leprosy were cured, evil spirits were cast out; even the dead were raised to life. People were amazed by what they saw and heard, and were attracted to him as a healer.

But how can we know that these miracles happened? Can we

accept the eyewitness testimony of many people? Should we believe in miraculous healing today? And are there any conditions that must be met before healing can occur? These are important questions that need to be asked when searching for the truth.

An Ethiopian proverb says, 'He who conceals his disease cannot expect to be cured.' The first step of any able physician is to determine the possible cause of the sickness. Then they endeavour to eliminate that cause. It is always necessary to recognize the root of the problem before full healing can occur. So it is when we approach God for healing. We discover that he deals less with symptoms than with causes. For that reason, it is appropriate to begin by considering some of the specific causes of disease.

People in Old Testament times often believed that disaster and disease were punishments for sin. That is why Eliphaz said to Job, *'Consider now: Who, being innocent, has ever perished? Where were the upright ever destroyed?'* (Job 4:7). Such reasoning was still prevalent amongst the early followers of Jesus.

The disciples of Jesus, when they saw a man afflicted with congenital blindness, asked who was responsible: *'Rabbi, who sinned, this man or his parents, that he was born blind?'* (John 9:2). To them, this blindness created a theological problem. Had this man sinned during his antenatal life in the womb, or was it the result of parental sin before his birth? Was he being punished because of the sins of others? And if so, was this fair? For those today who believe in reincarnation or transmigration, the man's condition would pose a further question. Did he sin in a previous life? The Bible, however, rejects such an idea. Each person dies only once and after that comes judgment (Hebrews 9:27).

Sin and sickness are closely associated in the Bible because God has pronounced just judgments upon the disobedient. Miriam, the prophetess, challenged the authority which God had assigned to Moses, her brother (Numbers 12). As a result Miriam suddenly became leprous, white as snow, and would have remained so had it not been for the intervention of Moses. He prayed earnestly for her deliverance, and God healed her. Obviously Miriam would not have needed healing if she had not sinned.

Paul deals with the subject of sickness among Christians in his letter to the Corinthians. He tells us that many people were 'weak and sick', and a number had died prematurely (1 Corinthians 11:30). God had clearly punished them because of their improper observance of the Lord's Supper. That is why Paul calls attention to their need of self-examination.

In some cases, a specific disease is due to a specific sin. Those people who seek happiness through the abuse of food, drink, drugs, tobacco, gambling, sex or other inappropriate behaviour are likely to suffer. They reap what they sow. It is certainly true that sin, due to the fall of humanity (Genesis 3; Romans 5:12), is the general cause for the existence of all sickness in the world. But it does not necessarily follow that an individual's personal suffering is attributable to their personal sin. Such a simplistic attitude is clearly dismissed by the life of Job. He was a blameless and upright man who feared God and stayed away from evil. Despite that, he lost his family, his wealth, and finally his health. And he was unable to understand why. He vociferously protested that his suffering and debilitating disease was out of proportion to his sinfulness. At the same time, his friends were quite certain that he must be guilty of some terrible sin. His friends did not believe that such bad things could happen to good people. They were wrong to deduce that every affliction is the direct result of a particular sin, and God leaves us in no doubt that they were wrong. Later, God 'made [Job] prosperous again and gave him twice as much as he had before' (Job 42:7–17).

Jesus diagnosed many physical ailments as the work of Satan (Mark 9:14–29; Luke 13:10–17). But he also identified some sickness as unrelated to personal sin. In the situation of the man born blind, we see that Jesus dismisses the man's personal sins and the sins of his parents as sources to which his blindness can be traced. Jesus says, '... *this happened so that the work of God might be displayed in his life*' (John 9:3). Hence, one reason for suffering is that God might intervene and demonstrate his power to heal.

Sometimes there are circumstances unknown to us for why people suffer, and so they are beyond our ability to trace. Job never knew the reason for why he suffered, but he reached a point where he believed that God knew and that was sufficient for him. He accepted that his questioning of God was wrong. Likewise we may have to accept that God has reasons for allowing suffering in our lives. He may share those reasons with us. He may reveal things that we could never have discovered by ourselves so that we might respond to them in a positive way. But whatever our circumstances, we must never attempt to tell him what he can or cannot do. God does not always answer us in the way we might like or expect. His decisions often surpass anything mere human beings could ever understand.

THE HEALING MINISTRY OF JESUS

Undoubtedly the ministry of Jesus was not only characterized by preaching and teaching the good news of the kingdom, but by healing as well. Jesus healed '*every disease and sickness among the people*' as he travelled throughout Galilee (Matthew 4:23). It appears here, and elsewhere, that healing was a common feature of his earthly ministry. Furthermore, no sickness or infirmity was too difficult for him to cure.

The Gospel writers emphasize that the healing miracles of

Jesus were motivated by compassion and mercy (Matthew 14:14; Mark 1:41; Luke 7:13–15). But the most important reason of all was that these miracles were authenticating signs of his divine nature and power. In John 20:30,31 we read, *'Jesus did many other miraculous signs in the presence of his disciples, which are not recorded in this book. But these are written that you may believe that Jesus is the Christ, the Son of God, and that by believing you may have life in his name.'* By his many miracles Jesus provided incontrovertible evidence that he was the prophesied Saviour sent from God (Isaiah 35:5,6). His miraculous healings showed that this was what God the Father wanted to do. Jesus said, *'I tell you the truth, the Son can do nothing by himself; he can do only what he sees his Father doing, because whatever the Father does the Son also does'* (John 5:19). His preaching, teaching and power were a visible manifestation of the kingdom of heaven. In spite of that, people responded to Jesus in extremely different ways. Some people loved Jesus, while others loathed him.

When Jesus was accused by the Pharisees of casting out demons by the power of Beelzebub, the prince of demons, he challenged them by stating a well-known fact of experience. *'Every kingdom divided against itself will be ruined, and every city or household divided against itself will not stand'* (Matthew 12:25). The Pharisees' slander against Jesus was tantamount to saying that Satan casts out Satan. Are they seriously suggesting that Satan would engage in activity that would inevitably destroy his own kingdom? Jesus concluded his defence with the positive statement that if he drove out demons by the Spirit of God, then the kingdom of God had arrived (Matthew 12:28). Obviously the kingdom of God was a present reality, not just a future hope.

There are several principles relating to the healing ministry of Jesus that ought greatly to influence a cynical and disbelieving public. For instance, he could heal diseases for which there was no known medical cure, and even the dead were commanded to get up. Of course, whatever the evidence, some people will argue against such miracles. Let us take, as an example, the healing of the man suffering from paralysis (Luke 5:20–26). Is it not possible that he suffered from a psychosomatic illness? Thus, if his paralysis didn't have a physical cause, he would be more susceptible to suggestion. The Bible, however, is quite clear that a remarkable healing took place that day in the house at Capernaum. That is why everyone was amazed by this awesome event and gave praise to God.

Another example that we might consider is the raising of the widow's only son that occurred just outside the Galilean town of Nain (Luke 7:11–17). Luke is the only New Testament writer to mention this incident, which appears to be a hopeless situation until Jesus, acting on his own initiative, touched the coffin. He commanded the young man to get up. Then the dead man sat up and began to talk, and Jesus gave him back to his mother. What are we to make of this? Did Jesus really bring the young man back from the dead? Or is it possible he wasn't dead in the first place, merely in a coma? Certainly for the large crowd of mourners who saw it happen there was no doubt that Jesus had brought the widow's son back to life. It is no wonder they were filled with awe and praised God. Luke, who was a doctor, was also convinced.

Jesus almost always healed people instantaneously, but on one occasion it happened in two stages (Mark 8:22–26). Some people brought a blind man to Jesus, with the request that he be healed. Jesus took the man by the hand and led him to some quiet place in the country. Then, spitting on the man's eyes, he laid his hands on him and asked, *'Do you see anything?'* The man replied, *'I see people; they look like trees walking around.'* So Jesus laid his hands on the man a second time, and the man's sight was fully restored. Why, we might ask, did the healing process not happen immediately? It is not possible to answer that question, for the reason has not been revealed to us. Undoubtedly the Bible sometimes presents us with facts that are beyond our comprehension. What is certain is that Jesus, who was able to raise the dead and who healed other blind people instantly, could easily have imparted instant recovery to this blind man. In spite of that, Jesus chose a way that was different and he must have had a very good reason for doing so. It should also be noted that the entire healing process, total blindness to perfect vision, was speedily accomplished. Otherwise the critics of Jesus could claim that the healing process was due to natural causes.

In Luke 4, we are told that Jesus left the synagogue and went to Simon Peter's home. Peter's mother-in-law was there, very sick with a high fever. At the request of those present, Jesus rebuked the disease and immediately her temperature returned to normal: 'She got up at once and began to wait on them' (v. 39). She was immediately healed and knew it.

The healing ministry of Jesus was always successful, whatever the illness. Whoever he touched was completely and permanently healed. There are no recorded instances of failure, partial recovery or of a relapse. Jesus unambiguously brought the healing power of God to the sick. Neither was it necessary for Jesus to have physical contact with the patient. We are told that a centurion, who was a high-ranking Roman soldier, sent a message to Jesus on behalf of his servant who was sick and about to die, 'Please come and heal him' (see Luke 7:1–10). Jesus immediately agreed to the request. But just before he arrived at the house, the centurion sent some friends to say, 'Lord, don't trouble yourself, for I do not deserve to have you come under my roof. That is why I did not even consider myself worthy to come to you. But say the word, and my servant will be healed' (vv. 6,7). The centurion, overwhelmed with a sense of unworthiness, had tremendous faith in the healing power of Jesus. As a result, the servant was healed without Jesus entering the centurion's house. In contrast, there is a royal official mentioned in John 4 who believed that Jesus could heal his son only by coming to him (vv. 46–53). He discovered that Jesus would not come. This man believed that Jesus could heal his son, but never thought that he could heal him at a distance. Despite his limited faith and slowness of understanding, his request was granted. Jesus told him to go back home: *'Your son will live.'* And the man believed, even though it was not until the next day that he realized that his son had indeed recovered.

Jesus did not reserve this healing ministry for himself, but passed it on to his twelve disciples. He *'gave them authority to drive out evil spirits and to heal every disease and sickness'* (Matthew 10:1). Healing was a meaningful part of their evangelism. They prayed, *'... enable your servants to speak your word with great boldness. Stretch out your hand to heal and perform miraculous signs and wonders through the name of your holy servant Jesus'* (Acts 4:29,30). Immediately God answered their prayers. Filled with the Holy Spirit they were enabled to perform many miraculous signs and wonders and to preach God's message with boldness.

It would be wrong to assume that healing was restricted to the twelve disciples. We are told that Stephen and Philip performed miraculous signs among the people in Jerusalem and Samaria (Acts 6:8; 8:6,7). Paul and Barnabas experienced the power of the Lord as they boldly proclaimed his name to the people of Iconium. The Spirit bore witness that their message was true by *'enabling them to do miraculous signs and wonders'* (Acts 14:3). Additionally there can be no doubt that the Holy Spirit gave some members of the infant New Testament church the ability to heal others (1 Corinthians 12:9,28). This raises the important question: Is there any evidence that the gift of miraculous healing is still given to certain believers?

SHOULD WE BELIEVE IN MIRACULOUS HEALING TODAY?

According to some advocates, there is nothing that cannot be miraculous healed. They believe that certain people or places have a close association with spiritual powers that enable them to cure diseases or heal disabilities. Therefore, healing is an accepted practice of several religious or 'spiritual' groups, as well as some branches of Christianity. Often it involves the healer touching or laying hands on the individual while praying to a supreme being. Alternatively, it may be practised at a distance, whereby one faith healer or a group of people will pray for the person. Sometimes faith healing will involve the patient making a pilgrimage to a religious place, such as the Catholic shrine at Lourdes, in hope of a miraculous recovery.

Before we go further, we should pause for a second to remember that not all healing is Bible-based or carried out in Jesus' name. 'Faith healing' does not always mean the faith being exercised is faith in the Lord Jesus, and may indeed be spiritualism. We must also remember that the influence of the mind over the body can result in remarkable healings. We should never underestimate the power of the psyche.

There are many people, including some Christians, who are disillusioned by modern claims of miraculous healing. The reason for this is that so often they appear to be based solely on sensationalism. Where, it might be asked, is the scientific evidence to support the claims that healing by faith and the laying on of hands can cure any illness and even raise the dead? Is it unreasonable to ask those who make these assertions to provide real, corroborated evidence to support their amazing claims? Sadly, we may discover that many of the alleged cures, following investigation, will turn out to be false. Occasionally, exhibitionist healers may use trickery and fraud to imitate the supernatural. As a result, people can be duped, losing their trust and their money.

For Christians in particular, false prophets may appear in the guise of charismatic healers, making extravagant but sadly often unsubstantiated claims regarding their achievements, promising miracles while asking for money. Some so-called healers may see it as something they can use to promote their own egos. They may boast about what they have done through their ministry and say considerably more about themselves than they do about Jesus Christ. This is the essence of ungodliness and a very clear warning that such people should be avoided.

Please understand that I am not saying all claims of miraculous healings are false. I know that is certainly not the case. God has the power to heal any physical affliction and even to raise those who have already died. He said, '*I am the* LORD, *the God of all mankind. Is anything too hard for me?*' (Jeremiah 32:27). No genuine Christian will deny this. Nevertheless, God does not always do what he can do but instead acts in accordance with his overall plan.

It does appear to me that most of the Christian healings that we hear about today are vastly different to those reported in the New Testament. Then the healings were unambiguously miraculous. For instance, those suffering from congenital blindness or paralysis were completely and instantaneously healed without any recorded instance of relapse. Now, however, we primarily hear about people being cured of aches or pains and so the authenticating evidence is much less convincing. There are extraordinary accounts of healing, especially from missionaries in developing countries, but these claims are more often than not difficult or impossible for us to verify. That is not to say, however, that they are false.

INSTRUCTIONS FROM JAMES

An important reference relating to the question of healing is to be found in the letter of James. In James 5:14,15 we find the following: *'Is any one of you sick? He should call the elders of the church to pray over him and anoint him with oil in the name of the Lord. And the prayer offered in faith will make the sick person well; the Lord will raise him up. If he has sinned, he will be forgiven.'* These instructions, although apparently straightforward, are often neglected or misunderstood by Christians today. Maybe this is due to the fact that they raise several very difficult questions rather than provide any undisputed answers. How should we interpret these two contentious verses that are so often used to support widely different practices?

It is sometimes suggested that these words written by James are a direct reference to Extreme Unction. This is a term used in the past but rarely used today for one of the seven sacraments, the sacrament of the Anointing of the Sick, which is practised by the Roman Catholic Church. The priest anoints with oil the person who is in *extremis*, that is, at the point of death, and prays for the remission of their sins. In sharp contrast, however, James refers to someone who is expected to live, and so it follows that there is no basis in using these verses to justify this sacrament.

Let us now look at a second possible answer which I also believe to be wrong. Namely, that what James says justifies divine healing ministries. There are many churches that place great emphasis upon the gifts of healing and set apart specific people for this task. A few are internationally famous and conduct large healing crusades. But does James justify such action? The answer is very simple. James makes no reference to anyone possessing 'a gift of healing' here. The sick person is to call for *the elders of the church* (v. 14). These were men who exercised leadership in pastoral oversight over the fellowship they represented. But we are nowhere told that these elders possessed 'the gift of healing' or of being able to perform miracles. The situation to which James refers is clearly an intimate and personal encounter within a local church, not a public display. Because the ill person is clearly bedridden (*'the Lord will raise him up'*, v. 15), the elders of the church, as a group, will bring the comfort and assurance of care and prayer. Thus there is no direct connection here to 'divine healing' ministries.

Jesus never organized healing crusades. Neither did he ever invite people to come and see the healings that would be performed. Quite the contrary! The arrival of many curious people led, not to a further display of miraculous healing, but to his leaving the scene. When he brought a young girl from death back to life, he refused the opportunity to draw attention to himself. Indeed, he gave strict orders to the family *'not to let anyone know about this'* (Mark 5:43).

Does fervent prayer offered in faith always make sick people well? There can only be one truthful answer: 'No!' It would seem that some people experience instantaneous and astounding healing while others are healed gradually. But what about those patients who continue to deteriorate and eventually die because of their illness? Is this because of a lack of faith? Is it because of unconfessed sin? How can we satisfactorily explain that what the Bible says is true, but in practice it does not always do what it appears to promise? The prayer offered in faith will make the sick person well, and yet God may choose not to restore someone to normal health. To answer this paradox we should note that the healing ministry to which James refers is subject to two factors: 1) the patient is anointed with oil *'in the name of the Lord '* (James 5:14), and 2) there must be *'prayer[s] offered in faith'* (v. 15).

Olive oil was a well-known medicine in antiquity. Isaiah 1:6 speaks of *'wounds and bruises and open sores'* being *'soothed with oil'*. The twelve apostles anointed many sick people with oil and healed them (Mark 6:13). In the parable of the good Samaritan, we read that oil and wine were applied to the wounds of the injured man (Luke 10:34). The oil would soothe and the wine, because of its alcoholic content, would act as a disinfectant and antiseptic. James, however, possibly does not mean to use oil just as an ordinary medicine, but rather as a symbolic outward sign of the healing to be brought about by God.

Elsewhere we see that what James says must not be misunderstood as an apostolic command to anoint all sick people with oil. The book of Acts provides many examples of how sick people were healed without the use of oil (3:6; 5:15,16; 9:34; 16:18). Neither did Jesus in his healing ministry resort to the use of oil. Anointing with oil is secondary to prayer and faith in the healing power of God.

The healing process described by James is only effective when done *'in the name of the Lord'*. Thus it is vital that there is a Spirit-directed conviction that it is God's will, in a particular instance, to heal. And, secondly, there must be *'prayer offered in faith'* That is, a prayer offered with the correct conviction that it has God's endorsement. '... *if we ask anything according to his will, he hears us'* (1 John 5:14). All faithful prayer is based on the theme *'your will be done'*. Jesus taught us to say this (Matthew 6:10) and provided the ultimate example of it in Gethsemane

(Matthew 26:39,42). This, incidentally, is the answer to those people who foolishly claim that everyone will be healed as long as they have sufficient faith. Prayer, if it is to be successful, must always accord with God's will.

WHEN GOD DOESN'T HEAL

Why God does or does not choose to heal is more often than not beyond our ability to fully understand. We have to accept that healing is ultimately subject to his wisdom and sovereign purposes. We cannot insist on healing as a right, and we must accept that it is not always God's will to make a sick person well. That is why even the great apostle Paul could not prevent the serious illness of Epaphroditus (Philippians 2:27). Neither could he heal Trophimus, who he had to leave sick in Miletus (2 Timothy 4:20). Why did not Paul pray in faith that his friends would be miraculously healed? I don't doubt that he did, but he learned from his own experience, when he urged the Lord to heal him, that requests are not always granted (2 Corinthians 12:8,9). There is no biblical guarantee of deliverance from sickness or many other problems in this life. Christians are saved from the penalty of sin, but not necessarily from suffering.

The Bible is quite clear that even in that charismatic period the apostles did not always receive power from the Lord to heal. Why then, we might ask, are there people today who insist that physical healing is God's will for all true believers? 'A good God would not allow anyone to suffer,' we are told by some. This, of course, is false. And how can anyone rightly say that if a person is not healed it must always be due to the fact that their faith is somehow deficient? Or that it is punishment because of unrighteousness? Obviously such an attitude, besides being incredibly insensitive and cruel, can cause serious problems. The person who is ill may experience feelings of failure, guilt, hopelessness and despair. There are those who will claim to have been miraculously healed, when they have not. Otherwise they fear it would imply that they lacked faith. Their problem is exacerbated because they not only have to cope with the original illness, but also with a sense of spiritual inadequacy. Likewise, the needs of the bereaved must also be taken into account. If they are led to believe that they have not exercised sufficient faith on behalf of the deceased, their grief will be all the more acute.

MEDICAL TREATMENT

Some advocates of Christian faith healing even go so far as to say that all conventional medical treatment must be avoided. That is a dangerous lie. Avoiding or delaying medical treatment may result in unnecessary suffering and even premature death. Why should we restrict God to working in supernatural ways without recourse to other means? Is not God able to heal a person in many different ways? Of course he can. God does not have to justify what he does or does not do.

There are numerous means by which God can restore our health, and we must never attempt to confine him to working in supernatural ways. God has created our bodies with a healing mechanism which is activated by illness or injury. That is a gift of God. The doctor's skill and medicines are gifts of God. Those people who claim that it is wrong to consult a doctor forget that Jesus said, *'It is not the healthy who need a doctor, but the sick'* (Matthew 9:12). Though Jesus was referring to the problem of sin, he was using an obvious analogy. Sick people should see a doctor. His words indicate that medical treatment is not contrary to the will of God. Paul, writing to the Colossians, refers to his *'dear friend Luke, the doctor'* (Colossians 4:14). Additionally he advised Timothy to '*Stop drinking only water, and use a little wine because of … [his] frequent illnesses*' (1 Timothy 5:23). Would not Paul have told him to call the elders if their ministry was the only God-honouring means of recovery?

HOLINESS

There are people who believe that health is the most important thing in life, but they forget that there is one thing that is far more important, and it is holiness. For that reason, Jesus came primarily not to physically heal the sick, but to save them from the penalty and power of sin. Alas, many people were attracted to Jesus only for the physical blessings he could bring, and not for the spiritual. This was a serious mistake. The state of our souls which continue to exist after physical death should concern us infinitely more than the state of our bodies. What use is perfect health in this life if we miss out on heaven in the next?

Hopefully what I have written in this chapter does not portray too negative a picture of miraculous healing. I am totally convinced that God heals, not only indirectly by means such as medical care, but also directly by his immediate intervention. Nor do I believe that people should resign themselves to sickness. Rather I am of the opinion that we should assume it is God's will to heal unless he makes it clear to us, as he did to Paul, that suffering is his will for someone at a particular time. God does not cause sickness, but he sometimes allows it so that his purposes will be fulfilled.

Paul, tells the Christians at Corinth that '*there was given me a thorn in my flesh*' (2 Corinthians 12:7). All kinds of suggestions have been made as to what this 'thorn' was but we don't really know. The word in the Greek is *skolops*, a sharply pointed stake, which indicates that it caused him a piercing pain in either his body or spirit. He three times pleaded with the Lord to heal him and his request was refused. Instead, Jesus answered him: '*My grace is sufficient for you, for my power is made perfect in weakness*' (2 Corinthians 12:9). There is no suggestion that Paul thought any less of God or of prayer because of his own experience. He readily accepted that God's grace would support him in every ordeal.

In the Old Testament, David prayed fervently for his baby son while he was alive; when the child died, David bowed in submission to the will of God (2 Samuel 12:15–23). David's response is a good example of how we should handle God's answer to prayer. We should never expect as a matter of course that God will answer all our prayers in the way we desire. Instead, he will answer in such a way as is most for his glory and our good.

If we are sick, we should pray about it, believing that God has the power to do anything he chooses; we should seek medical treatment, and we should accept that healing is because of unmerited mercy from a God who will act entirely in accordance with his sovereign, wise and perfect will. We need to remember that God sometimes chooses not to heal. Even so, whatever the outcome we need not worry, for God is always with us and understands our every need. What is the greatest need of every person on earth today? Is it physically healthy bodies? Certainly not! Forgiveness of sin is the greatest blessing that we can receive. The cross is a constant reminder of God's love and that those who believe in Christ can look forward to the perfect health that awaits them in the resurrection. Surely the afflictions of God's people are light and momentary when compared to the eternal joys of heaven that await them (2 Corinthians 4:17).

CHAPTER 4

ANGELS

What place do angels have in God's creation? What is their purpose? Who are these mysterious celestial creatures that are often confined to Christmas plays, religious cards, figurines and paintings? Do angels really exist? Or do they belong to the realms of fantasy? Does the Bible have anything to say about these questions? Yes, it does! The Bible has approximately three hundred references relating to angels and the experiences of people who encountered them. If you believe the whole Bible, you will certainly believe in angels and their ministry.

Angels were created by God, through Jesus Christ. *'For by him all things were created: things in heaven and on earth, visible and invisible ... all things were created by him and for him. He is before all things, and in him all things hold together'* (Colossians 1:16,17). This Creator, Jesus, is superior to created heavenly beings. They are subject to his control and dependent upon him for their continuing existence. The Bible leaves us in no doubt that angels should not, in any way, be worshipped (Revelation 22:8,9). It is not the things God made but the Creator alone who is to be praised forever (Romans 1:25).

The Bible is not specific about when the angels were created, I believe, so as not to distract us from God's plan of salvation for humankind. But it does reveal that they were present when God laid the foundations of the earth: '... *all the angels shouted for joy*' in response to God's creative work (Job 38:7). As a result, some people believe that the angels existed prior to the primary creation of heaven and earth, but such an assumption cannot be proved. The only certainty, based on such passages as Genesis 2:1,2 and Exodus 20:11, is that they were created before the seventh day.

WHAT IS AN ANGEL?

Our English word 'angel' comes from the Greek word *angelos*, which means an agent or messenger. The matching Hebrew word *mal'ak* has the same meaning. Angels are messengers of God who are sent out to accomplish his purposes. Through them God guides, encourages and protects his people, as we see in both the Old and New Testaments. The Bible also refers to a supreme angel, sometimes referred to as Lucifer, later called Satan, and other angels who became God's enemy. These fallen angels and their leader will be discussed in the next chapter.

The visual representations, abilities and duties of angels are diverse. Although they are essentially invisible spirit beings, they are also known to take on various visible forms for a specific service. Angels are known to have appeared as men on occasions. For example, one day about noon, as the patriarch Abraham was sitting at the entrance to his tent, he suddenly noticed three men standing nearby. He hurried to meet them, and bowed himself to the ground (Genesis 18:1,2). The following verses reveal that

Abraham provided a sumptuous meal for his guests, who later turned out to be a manifestation of God himself with two of his holy angels. These two angels, in the guise of men, next appear at Sodom. Abraham's nephew, Lot, who was sitting by the city gate, immediately stepped forward to offer them hospitality. This was initially refused, but because of Lot's insistence they finally accepted his invitation (Genesis 19:1–3).

In the New Testament we also see that angels appeared as men. The women who entered Christ's tomb saw what appeared to be a young man clothed in a white robe (Mark 16:5). Who was it? Matthew 28:5 says that it was an angel. Luke 24:4 describes the sudden appearance of two men clothed in dazzling robes, while John 20:11–13 refers to them as angels. It is clear that angels appear to humans in human form, and so an angel may also be called a man – they never appear as female in Scripture – and furthermore is able to express himself in human language. Paul refers to *'tongues ... of angels'* which suggests that they also speak their own language (1 Corinthians 13:1).

Although angels can appear in the form of men, they are different in numerous ways. For instance, human beings have a body and a spirit, which together form a unit. The spirit without the body is incomplete. In comparison, an angel is a spirit without a body, yet is complete.

God has given angels no ability to reproduce. Neither do they marry (Mark 12:25). Angels do not need rest (Revelation 4:8). It appears that angels do not become ill or grow old. Neither are good angels subject to death (Luke 20:36). Incidentally, that is what it will be like for people in their resurrected state in heaven, hard though it is to imagine. As there is no death in heaven, it follows that there will be no need for birth. Because angels are not limited to an earthly body, they are able to move instantly through space to perform their assignments. But despite the fact that they can appear, disappear and reappear with amazing rapidity they are, unlike God, not omnipresent. It is impossible for angels to be in two or more places simultaneously.

Angels are strong and powerful creatures. Just one angel rolled away a very large stone from the tomb of Jesus (Mark 16:4,5). Peter describes angels as being stronger and more powerful than men (2 Peter 2:11). He could speak from personal experience, having been miraculously released from prison by an angel (Acts 12:7–11). Paul, in 2 Thessalonians 1:7 refers to the *'powerful angels'* of God. From the Greek word *dunamis*, here translated 'powerful', we get the English word 'dynamite'. Angels can be likened to God's dynamite! Angels have the inherent ability to perform anything he commands. In Psalm 103:20, David speaks about the mighty angels who carry out God's plans. Yet, despite their mighty power, a power far superior to that of humans, it is secondary to that of God. Only God is omnipotent.

Another characteristic of the angels is that they possess knowledge superior to that of humankind. For instance, they witnessed God's creative work. Even so, vast as their knowledge is, angels do not know everything. Omniscience like omnipotence belongs only to God. Jesus bore witness to this fact when referring to his second coming. He said, 'No-one knows about that day or hour, not even the angels in heaven, nor the Son, but only the Father' (Matthew 24:36).

Angels, like ourselves, have free will and are thus capable of making mistakes. There is a passage in the book of Job which reveals that God charges his angels with error (4:18). Undoubtedly the greatest error for some was to join the satanic rebellion in heaven (2 Peter 2:4). In Jude's parallel account, the writer states that these angels '... did not keep their positions of authority but abandoned their own home' (v. 6). These rebellious angels are now living in spiritual darkness, awaiting the judgment of God from which they cannot escape.

HOW MANY ANGELS ARE THERE?

It is impossible to say for certain how many angels were created. Nevertheless, the Bible repeatedly leaves us in no doubt that their number is vast. David recorded *'tens of thousands and thousands of thousands'* (Psalm 68:17). Bildad, Job's friend, said many things that were wrong, but he was certainly right about there being a vast number of angels: *'Can his forces be numbered?'* (Job 25:3).

In the New Testament we are told that a great company of the heavenly host heralded the birth of Jesus to some terrified shepherds (Luke 2:8–14). Later, John tells us of having *'heard the voice of many angels, numbering thousands upon thousands, and ten thousand times ten thousand'*, praising the Lamb of God in the throne room of the universe (Revelation 5:11). We are presented here with a picture of an innumerable company of angels who continuously serve God without fatigue.

ARE THERE DIFFERENT TYPES OF ANGELS?

The Bible clearly reveals that not all angels are identical. One group which plays a prominent role is the cherubim, or cherubs. These angelic beings appear on the world stage as early as Genesis 3. God stationed cherubim at the entrance to the Garden of Eden so that re-entry for Adam and Eve was impossible (v. 24).

The prophet Ezekiel saw cherubim in a vision by the Kebar River. As he looked, he saw a great storm coming towards him from the north, driving before it an immense cloud that flashed with lightning and shone with brilliant light. The fire inside the cloud *'looked like glowing metal, and in the fire was what looked like four living creatures'* (Ezekiel 1:1–5). We know that these living creatures were cherubim because he later says: *'... the cherubim rose upwards. These were the living creatures I had seen by the Kebar River'* (10:15).

It is difficult, perhaps impossible, for us to adequately describe a vision of God in the language with which we are familiar. Ezekiel was no exception, and so he frequently resorts to phrases such as it 'looked like' or the 'appearance of'. Such bizarre imagery appears well-nigh incomprehensible to the finite human mind.

Each one of the cherubim had four faces and four wings (1:6). One face was like that of a man, the second the face of a lion, the third the face of an ox, and the fourth the face of an eagle (v. 10). Some interpreters suggest that the four faces portray the intelligence of humankind, the boldness of a lion, the strength of an ox and the swiftness of an eagle.

What else did Ezekiel see? He observed that *'Their legs were straight; their feet were like those of a calf and gleamed like burnished bronze'* (v. 7). Beneath each of their wings they had the hands of a man to serve. Each cherub travelled on what appeared to be a wheel intersecting a wheel. The rims of these wheels were awesomely tall and all four rims were full of eyes all around. They were able to move back and forth with the speed of lightning. Their appearance was brilliant like fire, and as they flew their wings made the noise like the roar of a great waterfall, or like the noise of the Almighty, or like the commotion of a mighty army. It is not surprising, then, that Ezekiel reacted by falling on his face in humility, awe and worship. He was completely overwhelmed by the greatness and glory of the incorruptible God (Ezekiel 1:7–28).

Sometimes in the Bible the cherubim were symbolic of heavenly things. At God's command there had to be two cherubim of hammered gold placed at the two ends of the atonement cover, which was above the Ark of the Covenant. These cherubim must face each other, looking down on the atonement cover with their wings outstretched above it (Exodus 25:18–22). Representations of the cherubim were also woven into or embroidered upon the Temple curtains (Exodus 26:1,31). Later, Solomon's Temple included cherubim in its decoration (1 Kings 6:23–29; 7:29,36; 8:6,7).

Another group of angels which play a prominent role are the seraphim, or seraphs. Their name is mentioned only in Isaiah 6:2,6 and means 'burning ones'. This probably indicates that their appearance is such that they seem as if they are on fire.

Seraphim have six wings, two of which cover their face, two of which cover their feet, and with the remaining two they fly. Covering their face was an expression of reverence and awe, inspired by the immediate presence of God. It also shielded their eyes from the one who dwells in *unapproachable light* (1 Timothy 6:16). Even the seraphim, despite being glorious creatures themselves, cannot look directly at God. Covering their feet was also an expression of reverence. What about their ability to fly? This reveals that they are equipped to readily respond to divinely assigned missions. We are not told how many seraphim there are, but the context appears to indicate a host.

Despite there being a vast number of angels, only two who serve God are actually named in Scripture. The first reference is to Gabriel. He appears four times by name and on each occasion serves as a messenger of good news to God's people. Twice he appeared to Daniel to interpret the meaning of his visions (Daniel 8:16; 9:21). Also Gabriel foretold the birth of John the Baptist (Luke 1:19) and the birth of Jesus (Luke 1:26).

The other angel mentioned by name is Michael who is

referred to three times in Daniel (10:13,21; 12:1), once in Jude (v. 9) and once in Revelation (12:7). Only Michael is designated as an archangel, but that is not to say that others do not belong to this order. Some Bible scholars quote Paul's reference to 'the archangel' (1 Thessalonians 4:16) to suggest that there is only one. Daniel 10:13, however, describes Michael as *one of the chief of princes.'* Does this indicate that there are multiple archangels? This question cannot be answered with any absolute certainty because Scripture does not say.

The word 'archangel' comes from a Greek word meaning chief angel. It is the highest rank in the celestial hierarchy. Yet even the archangel Michael, when he was disputing with the devil about the burial of Moses, did not dare to bring a slanderous accusation against him. He answered Satan, not in terms of his own authority, but simply said, *'The Lord rebuke you'* (Jude v. 9). Even though Michael ranked above Satan, it was God who must be the judge. How much more, then, should we avoid raising accusations against Satan and his cohorts. Rather we should pray the sixth petition of the Lord's Prayer, *'And lead us not into temptation, but deliver us from the evil one'* (Matthew 6:13).

THE ANGEL OF THE LORD

The 'messenger of Yahweh' or 'angel of the LORD' (*mal'ak* Yahweh) appears in the Old Testament on several occasions. But who is this angel? Is the 'angel of the LORD' different from all the other angels? The prevalent answer in evangelical Christianity is yes. As we turn the pages of the Old Testament, it appears that the 'angel of the LORD' is none other than a pre-incarnate appearance of Christ.

There is very strong evidence for accepting this belief as true. Nowhere is this clearer than when the 'angel of theLORD' claims to be God (Genesis 22:11–16; Exodus 3:2–6). Furthermore, some of those who saw this angel expressed great fear: '... *Moses hid his face, because he was afraid to look at God*' (Exodus 3:6). Gideon, when he finally realized that he had seen the 'angel of the LORD', feared for his life since no one could see God and live (Exodus 33:20). The LORD, however, immediately dispelled Gideon's fear by saying to him: 'Peace! Do not be afraid. You are not going to die' (Judges 6:23). Then Gideon built an altar to the LORD there and called it *'The LORD is Peace'* (v. 24) Obviously he would not have built an altar to angels or worshipped them. To do so would break the first commandment: *'You shall have no other gods before me'* (Exodus 20:3).

Further evidence is provided by the fact that what is applicable to God alone is attributed to the 'angel of the LORD.' He identifies himself with God. At the burning bush, he readily accepts worship from Moses (Exodus 3:5). If he was only an ordinary angel, regardless of stature, any act of worship would have been refused. Also the angel referred to in Exodus 23:20,21, who is generally considered to be the 'angel of the LORD', was able to forgive sins. This, again, is the exclusive right of God.

THE WORK AND MINISTRY OF ANGELS IN HEAVEN

The angels in heaven constantly surround the throne of God and continually rejoice in extolling his holiness. This is the only attribute of God in the Bible which is given a threefold emphasis: *'Holy, holy, holy is the LORD Almighty; the whole earth is full of his glory'* (Isaiah 6:3; see also Revelation 4:8). God is a God of utter holiness and therefore he cannot tolerate wrong.

Christ's sacrifice makes no provision for the angels who rebelled, and the holy angels need none (Hebrews 2:16). Nevertheless, the holy angels rejoice not only in God's work of creation (Job 38:7), but also in his work of salvation. John reveals that an innumerable company of angels encircle God's throne: *'In a loud voice they sang: "Worthy is the Lamb, who was slain, to receive power and wealth and wisdom and strength and honour and glory and praise!"'* (Revelation 5:12). The picture here is clearly one of triumph and exuberant joy because the resurrected Christ sits at the Father's right hand.

The vast army of God's angels, sometimes referred to as the host of heaven or heavenly host, are ever ready to obey his commands. He sends them on missions of love and justice, and they will gather his chosen ones at the time of Christ's return (Matthew 24:31; Mark 13:27). Throughout time there is an active angelic involvement on earth.

THE WORK AND MINISTRY OF ANGELS ON EARTH

Angels supported Jesus during his ministry on earth. For example, after he had fasted for forty days and forty nights and was physically weak, Satan three times in succession tried to tempt him in the wilderness. Three times Jesus quoted Scripture, and three times Satan failed. Then the devil went away, and angels came and cared for Jesus (Matthew 4:11). Following his victory, the angels provided Jesus with all that he needed. Their presence can also be seen as an act of homage.

Later, in the Garden of Gethsemane, an angel (Luke 22:43) helped sustain Jesus as he faced great suffering, death and separation from his Father the next day. Even with the presence of an angel, the anguish experienced by Jesus was so much that his sweat became like thick drops of blood falling down upon the ground. When Jesus was arrested, shortly after, he was not powerless. Had he wanted, he could have called on his Father and at once received the help of more than twelve legions of angels

(Matthew 26:53). None of the armed crowd would then have dared lay a hand on him. The fact is that Jesus laid down his life as a voluntary sacrifice so that the Scriptures would be fulfilled. Jesus totally submitted to the will of his Father. For our salvation he was crucified.

The angels that helped Jesus are also available to help us. Many stories are told by people of how God sent his angels to rescue them. In his motivational book *Touch the World through Prayer*, Wesley L. Duewel provides the following often quoted example:

During the Mau Mau uprising in Kenya in 1960, missionaries Matt and Lora Higgens were returning one night to Nairobi through the heart of Mau Mau territory, where Kenyans and missionaries alike had been killed and dismembered. Seventeen miles outside of Nairobi their Land Rover stopped. Higgens tried to repair the car in the dark, but could not restart it. They spent the night in the car, but claimed Psalm 4:8: 'I will lie down and sleep in peace, for you alone, O Lord, make me dwell in safety.' In the morning they were able to repair the car.

A few weeks later the Higgenses returned to America on furlough. They reported that the night before they left Nairobi a local pastor had visited them. He told how a member of the Mau Mau had confessed that he and three others had crept up to the car to kill the Higgenses, but when they saw the sixteen men surrounding the car, the Mau Mau left in fear. 'Sixteen men?' Higgens responded. 'I don't know what you mean!'

While they were on furlough a friend, Clay Brent, asked the Higgenses if they had been in any danger recently. Higgens asked, 'Why?' Then Clay said that on March 23, God had placed a heavy prayer burden on his heart. He called the men of the church, and sixteen of them met together and prayed until the burden lifted. Did God send sixteen angels to represent those men and enforce their prayers?[1]

I could quote many similar stories. Is it possible that they are all figments of the imagination? Could it be that what happened was due to a lucky coincidence or chance? Or were angels sent from God to aid his servants?

I believe in angels, not because of any obvious personal encounter. Neither am I unduly influenced by people today who claim to have experienced angelic help. I believe in angels and their intervention in human affairs because of what God says: '… *he will command his angels concerning you to guard you in all your ways*' (Psalm 91:11). I believe that God's Word is absolutely final.

We cannot read the Bible without becoming aware of the amazing role that angels have in protecting the lives of God's people. This is evident, for example, in the life of Elisha (2 Kings 6:1–17). He was in a place called Dothan that was well fortified but surrounded by many hostile Aramean soldiers. How would Elisha react to this situation? The answer is that he remained calm and confident, in contrast to his servant, who panicked. '"*Oh, my lord, what shall we do?" the servant asked. "Don't be afraid," the prophet answered. "Those who are with us are more than those who are with them."*' It appears that the servant was not easily calmed and so '… *Elisha prayed, "O LORD, open his eyes so that he may see." Then the LORD opened the servant's eyes, and he looked and saw the hills full of horses and chariots of fire all round Elisha.*' There was no way that anyone could capture Elisha or his servant.

It would be a mistake to see angels as a passing superstition present in the Old Testament, given the significant New Testament references. For example, Paul on his voyage to Rome faced shipwreck along with two hundred and seventy-five fellow passengers. A terrible storm had raged unabated for many days. The weather was so bad that it was impossible to see the sun by day and the stars by night. Thus, not surprisingly, the men gave up all hope. It was then that Paul calmly provided them with a much-needed word of encouragement. He had received assurance from an angel of God that no lives would be lost, but only the ship (Acts 27:23–26). God, through his angel, had said that all on the ship would be saved and so it could not be otherwise.

God not only protects and delivers his people, he also, through his angels, guides them. An angel went before Abraham's servant in finding a wife for Isaac (Genesis 24:7,40). An angel directed Philip to the desert road that ran from Jerusalem to Gaza so that he could meet an Ethiopian eunuch and lead him to Christ (Acts 8:26). Later, a Roman centurion called Cornelius saw in a vision an angel of God who told him to send some men to Joppa to find Simon Peter (Acts 10:3,7,22).

DO WE HAVE GUARDIAN ANGELS?

The belief that individual churches, or that each human being is assigned a specific angel, I believe, is a popular misconception. It is true that Jesus implied that God has assigned responsibility for the protection of 'little ones' to the care of his angels (Matthew 18:10). This does not, however, necessarily mean that each of God's children has a special guardian angel. Jesus may simply have been thinking of the protective roles angels have in keeping watch over believers.

In Acts 12:13–15, we read, 'Peter knocked at the outer entrance, and a servant girl named Rhoda came to answer the door. When she *recognised Peter's voice, she was so overjoyed she ran back without opening it and exclaimed, "Peter is at the door!" "You're out of your mind," they told her. When she kept insisting that it was so, they said, "It must be his angel."'* This probably reflects a Jewish belief that each person has a guardian angel that can assume the person's appearance and thus serve as their double. Obviously there were some, even among the disciples, who believed this to be true. Despite that, we cannot justify such a belief. What is certain is that God uses his angels as ministering spirits and may assign individual angels, or several angels, for specific duties on our behalf at any given time (Psalm 91:11; Hebrews 1:14).

Although God assigns angels to work on our behalf, it is not unknown for their protective care to be withdrawn. For example, two angels brought Lot, his wife, and his two daughters out of wicked Sodom before it was destroyed by fire (Genesis 19:15–26). Lot's wife, however, deliberately disobeyed the specific instructions of the angel and looked back towards Sodom (v. 17). She was reluctant to leave her earthly possessions and so the angels could not help her. As a result she was suddenly struck dead and her body became encrusted with salt (v. 26).

If we are obedient, God orders his angels to protect us wherever we go. Now, I know that this does not always appear to be so. When tragedies happen, many of us ask, 'Where were God's angels?' The answer is that unseen forces are at work in the spiritual realm. We may even see angels and fail to recognize them. That being so, the writer of Hebrews tells us not to forget to entertain strangers, for some who have done this have entertained angels without being aware of it (13:2). The very same thing that happened to Abraham and Lot cannot be ascribed to them exclusively. God is able to send his angels in human form whenever and wherever he desires. Therefore, as

God's servants, we can take great comfort in knowing that we have an undefeatable spirit army on our side.

NOTES

1. Wesley L. Duewel, Touch the World through Prayer (Grand Rapids, MI: Zondervan, 1986).

CHAPTER 5

THE ANGELIC
REBELLION

The Bible clearly defines two groups of angelic messengers: some are described as good or elect, and others as evil or fallen. The good angels continually praise God, serve him faithfully, and aid his people. These angels have never sinned. In sharp contrast, the evil angels, under their new master, Satan, are in constant revolt against God and will do all within their power to thwart his work. Their primary aim is to mislead and encourage sinners in their evil ways and cause their eternal separation from God. Undoubtedly the greatest catastrophe ever to occur was Satan's defiance of God, and the rebellion of the angels – as many as one third (Revelation 12:4) – who chose to follow him.

WHEN DID THESE ANGELS SIN?

The Bible does not reveal the exact time that Satan and some of the other angels sinned. Therefore, other than to say that it was sometime prior to the temptation of Adam and Eve in Paradise, we ought not to speculate. The vital question is not, 'When did these angels sin?' but the fact that 'Some angels fell because they sinned against God'.

Time and again I have been asked, 'How could a holy God create something sinful?' The answer is that he did not. *'God saw all that he had made, and it was very good'* (Genesis 1:31). Indeed, the entire work of creation that had now been completed was perfect. Even Satan was created as a good angel, but he failed to retain his exalted position.

This raises several difficult questions. For instance, why did God, who is almighty and holy, allow Satan and many other angels to sin? How can any being that was very good do that which was evil? How can we explain the origin of evil? Then, following the angelic rebellion, why did God not immediately destroy them? God knew that Satan would continue his rebellion by destroying people's bodies and souls. Therefore, why did God allow the opposition against him and humankind to continue? The same question can be asked of virtually any evil action. Why does God not stop it?

It is not possible for us to give a totally satisfactory answer to every question relating to God and his ways, nor is there any need to know. One thing is surely clear; God did not create evil. The psalmist says, *'As for God, his way is perfect'* (Psalm 18:30). Thus, we must accept that the perfect plan of our perfect God was to allow sin. Had he not done so, both angels and humans would be serving God out of obligation, not choice. To do what God demands only because one cannot do otherwise has no moral value. Hence, God allowed for the possibility of evil so that his created beings could have a free will to choose whether or not they wanted to serve him.

The Bible reveals that some of the angels fell from the perfect state in which they were created and that they will be condemned. Moreover, unlike humans (Romans 6:23), rebellious angels cannot repent and be forgiven. Their rebellion, considering what they knew about God, was the pinnacle of evil. Accordingly, they are forever banned from God's glory and presence: '... *God did not spare angels when they sinned, but sent them to hell, putting them into gloomy dungeons to be held for judgment*' (2 Peter 2:4). In Jude's parallel account, we are told that these angels '... *did not keep their positions of authority but abandoned their own home – these he has kept in darkness, bound with everlasting chains for judgment on the great Day*' (v. 6). Peter and Jude do not reveal who these angels were, or the nature of their sin, but they do warn us that no created being is beyond the reach of God's justice.

HOW DID THESE ANGELS SIN?

The idea that angels could fall leads us to ask: 'What kind of sin can an angel commit?' There are scholars who believe that some of the angels fell as a result of them cohabiting with women. They usually base their argument upon Genesis 6:2 where it says, '*the sons of God saw that the daughters of men were beautiful, and they married any of them they chose.*' Also it resulted in the birth of children who were giants, which is how Nephilim is sometimes translated.

We need to ask ourselves a question here. Are the 'sons of God' angels? In the book of Job (1:6; 2:1; 38:7) this designation definitely refers to angels. There are, however, other instances in the Old Testament where people are referred to as 'sons of God'. For example, Hosea 1:10 mentions 'sons of the living God' in reference to Israel.

How, then, should we interpret Genesis 6:2? Is it about unnatural relationships between women and angels? Or should it be seen as a reference to human beings? To suggest the former is, I believe, untenable. Such an interpretation would be contrary to the spiritual nature of angels and, as Matthew 22:30 reveals, angels do not marry. Furthermore, if this interpretation was true it would mean that a twofold fall of angels occurred: the original plus this, the second. Thus, it appears more likely that the 'sons of God', that is God-fearing people, married the beautiful daughters of their ungodly neighbours and so forfeited their distinctiveness, with devastating consequences.

Sometimes it is suggested that certain angels rebelled because God had told them that he would create humankind, that they would sin against him, and that his Son would redeem those who repented. Moreover, all of the angels would be required to serve Christ in his humanity and to serve as ministering spirits to humankind. Satan and those who followed him could not accept this. They considered it to be demeaning, and rebelled.

It is impossible and unnecessary for us to know the precise details relating to Satan's fall. All that can be said with any certainty is that the basis of their sin was pride (1 Timothy 3:6). Of all the sins, none is more repugnant to God than pride: *'The LORD detests all the proud of heart. Be sure of this: They will not go unpunished'* (Proverbs 16:5). Pride, the result of a high or overbearing opinion of one's worth or importance, leads to the failure of a created being to realize who God is and that he alone is worthy of praise and worship. Satan had no desire to worship or obey God; he desired to be God.

Isaiah 14:12 says, *'How you have fallen from heaven, O morning star* ('*Lucifer*', King James Version), *son of the dawn! You have been cast down to the earth, you who once laid low the nations!'* This verse is the cause of much controversy. Sometimes Lucifer, the most bright and beautiful of all creatures in heaven, is considered to be the name Satan bore prior to his fall. There are, however, those who strongly reject this idea.

It is not unreasonable to ask how Lucifer, a Latin name, could find its way into a Hebrew manuscript. The name is derived from the words *lux*, 'light or fire' and *ferre*, to bring. Hence, Lucifer means 'light bringing', suggesting that he was of a very high rank among the angels. Lucifer is also one of the names for the morning star, Venus. When Jerome translated the biblical manuscripts in his Latin Vulgate, he used the term 'Lucifer', which meant Venus, to translate 'morning star'. The translators of the King James Bible used Jerome's translation for Isaiah 14:12 and Lucifer, although almost every translation since has removed it, became a part of the English language.

As we examine Isaiah 14:3–23, we see that it concerns the pride, splendour and fall of the king of Babylon. But is that the whole story? Is the prophet Isaiah only saying that the king of Babylon was evil? Maybe Babylon's king, in seeking to deify himself, copies Satan and is a 'type' of the Antichrist (Daniel 11:36; 2 Thessalonians 2:4). Additionally it could be said that his great humiliation is indicative of Satan's fall. Or are we to understand these verses as a direct reference to the fall of Satan? If the latter is true, then the five 'I will' declarations, found in Isaiah 14, depict the sin of Satan and reveal his rebellion and desire to be like God:

I will ascend to heaven;
I will raise my throne above the stars of God;
I will sit enthroned on the mount of assembly ...
I will ascend above the tops of the clouds;
I will make myself like the Most High.

(vv. 13,14)

The following verses from Ezekiel 28:11–19 may also have a double meaning. Do they refer only to an earthly king, the king of Tyre? Or do they describe Satan as someone who was full of wisdom, beauty and splendour in the beginning, but who later became corrupted by pride? Ezekiel says:

> *You were the model of perfection, full of wisdom and perfect in beauty …*
> *You were anointed as a guardian cherub …*
> *You were blameless in your ways from the day you were created till wickedness was found in you.*
>
> (28:12,14,15)

Even if we accept the passages in Isaiah and Ezekiel as having double meanings, the Bible still tells us very little about the fall of Satan and the angels who followed him. What we do know is that the rebellion failed. Revelation 12:7–9 vividly describes the downfall of Satan and his allies as follows: '*And there was war in heaven. Michael and his angels fought against the dragon, and the dragon and his angels fought back. But he was not strong enough, and they lost their place in heaven. The great dragon was hurled down – that ancient serpent called the devil, or Satan, who leads the whole world astray. He was hurled to the earth, and his angels with him.*'

SATAN – TITLES AND DESCRIPTIONS

The word 'satan' originally meant simply an 'adversary', and so does not necessarily refer to a wicked being. Satan, in the Bible, is a word often used to describe ordinary people. 1 Kings 5:4 reveals that Solomon, at the beginning of his reign, was so blessed by God that there was no adversary (Hebrew word *satan*) against him. But later, 1 Kings 11:14,23, the kings Hadad and

Rezon both became his adversaries, satans. The Philistines were suspicious that David would be their satan (1 Samuel 29:4). Even the angel of the LORD who stood in the road to oppose Balaam because of his wilful sin can be called a satan, an adversary to him (Numbers 22:22).

Matthew 16:22,23 provide another example. Peter could not accept that Jesus must go to Jerusalem to die on the cross. He failed to realize that without the crucifixion there could be no resurrection: *'"Never, Lord!" he said. "This shall never happen to you!"'* Jesus immediately replied, *'Get behind me, Satan!'* Peter was acting as an adversary, a stumbling block to Jesus.

Since satan means simply an adversary, it follows that a good person, even God himself, can be called a satan. Why, then, do we associate the word 'satan' with sin? The answer is very simple. It is due to the fact that our own sinful nature is our greatest adversary, or satan. But how can God be a satan? He can be a satan to us by bringing trials into our lives, or by preventing us from going astray. Job, after experiencing many severe trials, said to God, *'You turn on me ruthlessly; with the might of your hand you attack me'* (Job 30:21). Basically he was saying, 'God, you are acting as a satan against me.' However, this does not in any way suggest that God is sinful.

Although satan is widely used to describe people in the Old Testament, it also, of course, appears as a proper name for the malignant enemy of God and his people. This can be seen in the story of Job, a man who was blameless, a man of complete integrity. He feared God and stayed away from evil. Yet in spite of that, God allowed Job to be tested so that his good character could be proved.

Satan's desire was to try to make Job renounce his God. Hence, Satan is the counsel for the prosecution against Job. The slanderous accusation is that Job only serves God because of the blessings he has received. Take away everything Job has, and his loyalty will surely cease (Job 1:6–12; 2:1–6). Likewise, Satan is the counsel for the prosecution against the high priest Joshua, whose filthy garments God changed for clean ones (Zechariah 3:1). And Satan was the agitator behind David's sin (1 Chronicles 21:1). Satan always hates God and his people and will do all that he can to create a barrier between believers and their redeemer. He accuses them before God day and night (Revelation 12:10). In every age it has been the same.

The New Testament describes Satan in numerous ways. In the book of Revelation he is twice referred to as *'The ... dragon ... that ancient serpent called the devil, or Satan'* (12:9; see 20:2). Obviously the use of the title 'dragon' is symbolic because no such monster exists among the beasts of the earth. Nevertheless, it aptly describes Satan's great power and ferocious, murderous nature. He is also identified with the 'ancient serpent,' who by malicious craftiness, deceived Eve into disobeying God's commands and thus introduced sin into the world (Genesis 3). As a result, Satan is often portrayed in art and literature as a serpent or dragon. His title 'the devil' is derived from the Greek word *diabolos*, literally an accuser or slanderer.

Jesus, at crucial stages of his life, is challenged by a personal devil. For instance, following his baptism he was led by the Holy Spirit into the mountainous wilderness of Judea to be tempted there by the *diabolos*; that is, the devil. The first Adam had succumbed to temptation and now it was time to conquer the Son of God, the last Adam (1 Corinthians 15:45). But what succeeded in Eden, the perfect environment, failed in the wilderness. Both Matthew (4:1–10) and Luke (4:1–12) report three specific attacks to divert Jesus from his mission, and each time he meets them with a word of Scripture: '*It is written...* ' Jesus knew throughout with whom he was dealing, and called the adversary by his personal name, Satan (Matthew 4:10).

Devil is also used as a personal attribute. Jesus said, '*Have I not chosen you, the Twelve? Yet one of you is a devil!*' (John 6:70). He was speaking about Judas, the son of Simon Iscariot. The word 'devil' here simply refers to a wicked man.

John 12:31 speaks of Satan as '*the prince of this world*' and Matthew 12:24 as '*the prince of demons*'. Matthew also calls him the '*tempter*' (4:3) and '*the evil one*' (13:19). He is '*the accuser*' (Revelation 12:10). The apostle Paul refers to him as '*the ruler of the kingdom of the air*' (Ephesians 2:2). He also says, '*What harmony is there between Christ and Belial?*' (2 Corinthians 6:15). The name 'Belial' means 'worthlessness' or 'hopeless ruin'. Satan is a '*murderer*' and '*the father of lies*' (John 8:44). It was because of Satan's lies that sin entered the world and robbed us of the original gift of eternal life (Romans 5:12).

'Beelzebub' or 'Beelzebul,' Greek '*Beelzeboul*' are also names applied to Satan (Matthew 12:24). Probably they are a variant of 'Baal-Zebub' (2 Kings 1:2,3,6), the Edomite god of flies who was considered to possess the power to send or avert plagues. The reason for the different New Testament spelling is unclear. According to some commentators the name can mean 'lord of the flies' (as used by William Golding in the title of his book), or 'lord of dung'. Either of these are names of reproach and uncleanness and therefore applicable to Satan. Other commentators believe it should be translated 'lord of the abode', thus identifying Satan as the god of demon possession. Whatever interpretation we accept, it is clearly a reference to 'the prince of demons' that is, Satan.

The above list of names is far from exhaustive. Even so, it does give us a better understanding of the many roles Satan plays, and of his method of operation.

SATAN'S ACTIVITIES

Jesus taught that the world in which we live is not the kingdom of God but the kingdom of Satan. That is why there is so much evil in the world. Satan continuously attempts to discredit God's work, and he does this in many different ways. His onslaught may be physical, through persecution; it may be intellectual, through false teaching; or it may be moral, by promoting unethical standards. Furthermore, he is capable of changing tactics with bewildering speed. Let this be a stern warning to us all!

We learn much about Satan's cunning activity and how to respond to him by studying the temptation of Eve in the Garden of Eden (Genesis 3:1–5). He begins by instilling doubt about what God actually said: *'Did God really say, "You must not eat from any tree in the garden"?'* Satan then tries to substitute his own word for that of God: *'You will not surely die.'* This principle is clearly illustrated in the first two parables of Matthew 13. The parable of the sower, or to be more accurate, the parable of the soils; followed by the parable of the weeds. Good seed, which is the Word of God, becomes mixed with Satan's lies and produces a harvest of corruption.

Finally, Satan questions God's motive. He says, *'For God knows that when you eat of it your eyes will be opened, and you will be like God, knowing good and evil.'* Has God enforced a restraint upon her freedom of choice and the increase of her knowledge? Can it possibly be that God's purpose was to prevent her from enjoying something of tremendous worth?

Instead of saying: 'Away from me, Satan!' Eve, like everyone since, succumbed to temptation. The forbidden fruit was pleasing to the eye. It appealed to Eve's sense organs. Satan's strategy is always to make that which is sinful appear to be desirable. That is what happened here and so, despite the unambiguous command of God, she took some of the fruit and ate it. She also gave some to her husband, who was with her, and he ate it too. There can be pleasure in sin. Otherwise people would not commit it. The problem is that the pleasure does not last. Sin inevitably leads to sadness or bitterness.

It is the same today as it was with Adam and Eve. Satan's tactics do not change. He appeals to our bodily senses and emotional nature. That is how Jesus was attacked in the desert following his baptism (Matthew 4:1–11). Satan first tried to seduce Jesus into abusing his power so as to provide food. He said, *'If you are the Son of God, tell these stones to become bread'* (v. 3). Jesus, after having fasted for forty days and forty nights, was very hungry. As a result, would he succumb to temptation as the first Adam had done? No, despite his pangs of hunger, Satan's temptation failed. Quoting Deuteronomy 8:3, Jesus answered, *'Man does not live on bread alone, but on every word that comes from the mouth of God.'* Satan's first attack had failed, but he did not give up.

Next, Jesus was taken to the *'holy city'*, that is, Jerusalem. If he is so convinced that nothing is beyond God's power, then surely he can prove this by throwing himself from the highest point of the Temple and survive? Satan even had the audacity to quote from Scripture, though out of context, as part of his temptation: *'He will command his angels concerning you, and they will lift you up in their hands, so that you will not strike your foot against a stone'* (v. 6; see Psalm 91:11,12). Immediately Jesus exposed Satan's tactics as a misuse of Scripture, and quoted Deuteronomy 6:16: *'Do not put the Lord your God to the test.'* It would be wrong to perform a miracle so as to satisfy an attitude of unbelief.

By taking an isolated portion of Scripture, and ignoring the context in which it appears, it is possible to justify almost anything you like. It is a well-founded saying that a text without a context can become a pretext. Hence, a basic principle to be borne in mind when interpreting Scripture is to consider the circumstances in which it was written. Failure to observe this rule will often result in wrong, even ludicrous, interpretations. The Bible is its own best interpreter and so, like Jesus, we should always compare Scripture with Scripture.

The third temptation of Jesus came when Satan showed him all the kingdoms of the world and their splendour. '*"All this I will give to you,"* he said, *"if you will bow down and worship me"*' (Matthew 4:9). Would this man, Jesus, succumb to such an offer? Would he remain faithful to the plan of his heavenly Father and experience shame, agony, and the cross? Or would he take the easy road, and worship Satan? The answer is that Jesus overcame this temptation by again quoting from the book of Deuteronomy: 'Worship the Lord your God, and serve him only' (v. 10; see Deuteronomy 6:13).

Had Jesus yielded to any of the above temptations, his whole life's mission would have failed. But, full of the Holy Spirit, he successfully resisted all of these attacks. No human or spiritual powers could take his life from him until he was ready to lay it down willingly for the sins of the world. And his time had not yet come.

Finally, having exhausted his temptations, and realizing his defeat, Satan went away. Even so, it should also be noted that this was only '*until an opportune time*' (Luke 4:13). We should never assume that success against one attack guarantees immunity from any other.

It is often asked if Satan had the authority to offer all the nations of the world to Jesus or anyone else. Satan says that they are his to give to anyone he pleases (Luke 4:6). This claim, of course, is a lie. Satan is not the ultimate ruler of the nations. He did not create them and neither is he in a position to dispose of them as he pleases, for he is subject to God. Satan does only what God permits (Job 1:12). Even if the nations had been his to give, he would not have kept his promise. Jesus specifically warns us that Satan is a liar (John 8:44).

In *Expository Thoughts on John*, J.C. Ryle, the first Bishop of Liverpool, stressed this fact when he wrote:

> There is a devil! ... He is ever going about, seeking whom he may devour. – He is a liar! He is continually trying to deceive us by false representations, just as he deceived Eve at the beginning. He is always telling us that good is evil and evil is good, – truth is falsehood and falsehood truth, – the broad way good and the narrow way bad. Millions are led captive by his deceit, and follow him, both rich and poor, both high and low, both learned and unlearned. Lies are his chosen weapons. By lies he slays many.[1]

We must always respond to the lies of Satan as Jesus did, with the truth of God's Word.

Satan deceives people, as we see, for example, in Paul's second letter to the Corinthians. The apostle Paul was constantly plagued by individuals who disagreed with him. He ignored many of them but certainly challenged those who were a threat to the fundamental beliefs of the church. He likened such critics to the tempter in the Garden of Eden. His great concern was that just as Eve was deceived by the serpent, the Christians in Corinth would be led away from their pure and simple devotion to Christ

(2 Corinthians 11:3). Then, so as to prevent any misunderstanding, he calls his critics *'false apostles, deceitful workmen, masquerading as apostles of Christ. And no wonder, for Satan himself masquerades as an angel of light'* (2 Corinthians 11:13,14). A major weapon of Satan in his warfare against the church is false teaching. That is why deceivers who preach their own insidious version of Christianity or a materialistic philosophy exist in every generation.

Satan, besides instigating sin by malicious lies, is also by divine permission capable of inflicting bodily disease and infirmity upon God's people. One book in the Bible makes that very clear, and that is the book of Job. In Job 2:7 we read, *'So Satan went out from the presence of the* LORD *and afflicted Job with painful sores from the soles of his feet to the top of his head.'* Satan tried to make him curse God. However, in all of this, Job did not sin by blaming God.

Illness is a way that Satan may sometimes use to draw us away from God. We must accept that Christians may suffer such severe trials and not experience instant healing. Yet, in spite of that, Christians can rest assured in the fact that God is in control.

Ultimately Satan desires to ruin human bodies and souls. The Bible speaks of people being possessed by 'devil[s]' or 'evil or unclean spirits'. In some instances the demon possession causes physical ailments, such as epileptic symptoms. We see this, for example, in Luke 9:37–43. A man was in great distress because his only son was controlled by a demon and suffering both in body and soul. Even while Jesus was speaking to this man, the demon threw the boy to the ground in a convulsion. This was not an ordinary case of epilepsy. Jesus unhesitatingly drove out the evil spirit, healed the boy and gave him back to his father.

It is important to note that demon possession and mental or physical illness are different and must never be confused. On the other hand, especially in Western cultures, Satan's involvement in afflicting people is often not considered seriously enough. Satan and his associates are always active. Therefore exorcism, although I believe it to be a specialist ministry, is still relevant today, as we shall see in the next chapter.

The real battle, for Jesus, was not between him and the Pharisees, or any other group of people, it was between Jesus and Satan. It is Satan and his underlings who tempt human beings into rebellion against God. However, although we face ferocious opposition, we may take encouragement from the fact that Satan and his underlings are creatures both of space and time. Despite their power, they are no match for God the Creator. The apostle Paul, after having spoken about affliction, distress and persecution, emphasizes that Christians are more than conquerors. He is sure 'that neither death nor life, neither angels nor demons, neither the present nor the future, nor any powers ... will be able to separate us from the love of God that is in Christ Jesus our Lord' (Romans 8:38,39). The evil of the world need never overwhelm us, for God is our helper.

NOTE

1. J.C. Ryle, *Expository Thoughts on John* (Edinburgh: Banner of Truth Trust, 1987).

CHAPTER 6

DEMON POSSESSION AND OCCULT PRACTICES

The New Testament contains several accounts of Jesus casting out demons. Exorcism was an integral part of his ministry. In Mark 5:1–20 and Luke 8:26–39 we read about Jesus being met by a demon-possessed man (two such men, according to Matthew 8:28). The demoniac (or demoniacs) addressed Jesus as follows: *'What do you want with me* [or us], *Jesus, Son of the Most High God?'* The demons, and in this instance there were many, were afraid that Jesus had come to torment them. 'Send us into those pigs feeding on the hillside nearby,' they begged. So Jesus gave them permission. As a result the entire herd of about two thousand pigs, now demon possessed, rushed down the steep hillside into the lake, where they drowned. Why did Jesus allow this to happen? As I see it, the primary reason was to show that Jesus values a human life more than many animals. We should not be surprised by this because humankind is made in the image of God; the pigs are not. It is this fact which throws true light upon the situation. People are important to God; otherwise he would have destroyed them as a punishment for their rebellious nature. But instead, the amazing truth is that those who trust in Jesus Christ for forgiveness are looked upon as though they have never sinned.

It is very clear from the above instance that the only satisfactory solution to demon possession was, and still is, demon expulsion. There can be no natural solution to a supernatural problem. Demons are not afraid of physical or psychological treatments applied over any length of time. Human power cannot do anything to control them. That is why, prior to Jesus, all attempts to conquer these demons had invariably failed.

Sometimes the influence of demons caused serious physical ailments. It caused muteness; for *'when the demon was driven out, the man who had been mute spoke'* (Matthew 9:33). In Matthew 12:22 we read of a demon-possessed man who was blind and unable to speak. Jesus healed him, so that as a result he could both see and talk. And then in Mark 9:14–27, a father describes his son's illness as what appears to be a case of epilepsy. The poor child had experienced frequent seizures, foaming at the mouth, gnashing his teeth, and rigidity. Additionally, he was unable to speak or hear. This is not an ordinary case of epilepsy, for it is clear from what we are told that the illness was caused by 'a spirit'; that is, the boy was demon possessed. The boy's father thought that Jesus may be able to help, but he is not certain. He says, '... *if you can do anything, take pity on us'* Of course Jesus can help. Jesus says to him, *'Everything is possible for him who believes'* (v. 23). Immediately the father believed and Jesus rebuked the evil spirit: *'"You deaf and mute spirit," he said, "I command you, come out of him and never enter him again." The spirit shrieked, convulsed him violently and came out. The boy looked so much like a corpse that many said, 'He's dead.' But Jesus took him by the hand and lifted him to his feet, and he stood up'* (vv. 25b–27).

Jesus also gave his twelve apostles, as part of their commissioning, the power and authority to drive out all demons and to cure diseases. They had never done this before. Neither was there any way that they could do any of these things by themselves. It was Jesus who gave them the *'power and authority'* necessary for their urgent and important mission as his official ambassadors (Luke 9:1). He sent them out to tell people about the coming of the kingdom of God. They also cast out many demons and healed many sick people. Even so, they were not given this authority unconditionally. In Luke 9:40, we read of an occasion when they had not been able to drive out an evil spirit. In spite of what they had seen Jesus do, and of the promise they had been given by him, they could still be influenced by unbelief.

It would be a mistake to believe that this power was only granted to the Twelve. For instance, Jesus later commissioned seventy-two others (Luke 10:1). Some manuscripts differ as to whether there were seventy or seventy-two, but we should not be unduly concerned about this. Considerably more important is the fact that Jesus instructed and empowered this group to heal and to preach. How long it took them to accomplish their mission and where they met Jesus on their return has not been revealed, nor is there need to know. What we do know is that they were evidently successful. *'The seventy-two returned with joy and said, "Lord, even the demons submit to us in your name"'* (Luke 10:17).

The seventy-two were elated by the success of their first mission. But following a time of success, there often lies a time of great danger. Hence, Jesus reminds them that he had seen *'Satan fall like lightning from heaven'* (Luke 10:18). He may have said this to put their achievements in perspective, or maybe it was to warn them against pride, which resulted in Satan's downfall. Jesus also reminded them that the power and the right to exercise that power had been given to them by him (v. 19). It was undoubtedly a tremendous privilege to be allowed to cast out demons and perform other mighty works. Yet it was a much greater privilege that their names were registered as citizens of heaven (v. 20).

It was not only the acknowledged disciples of Jesus who could expel demons. For this reason John said to Jesus: *'we saw a man driving out demons in your name and we told him to stop, because he was not one of us'* (Mark 9:38). Notice the word 'us'. They told him to stop because he wasn't in one of their groups. Had John and his companions acted appropriately? They thought so at the time, but were they now doubtful? Were they resentful of this man's success? Maybe they expected to be commended by Jesus; instead, he corrected them. *'"Do not stop him," Jesus said. "No-one who does a miracle in my name can in the next moment say anything bad about me, for whoever is not against us is for us"'* (vv. 39,40). This man, because of his personal faith in Jesus, had attained the power to drive out demons. Jesus stated that one of the specific signs of God's kingdom being evidenced on earth would be the driving out of demons (Matthew 12:28; Luke 11:20).

Occasionally, we may hear people say that the demonic references in the New Testament are simply the old way of referring to insanity. Thus it is important to stress that demon possession and mental or physical illnesses and abnormalities are totally different and separate things and must never be confused. They require separate diagnosis and different treatment. For example, Mark 6:13 says, *'They drove out many demons and anointed many sick people with oil and healed them.'* Demon possession is distinguished from ordinary ailments, and therefore exorcism from healing.

CAN A CHRISTIAN TODAY PERFORM AN EXORCISM?

Several different answers are frequently given to the above question. First, there are many people who do not believe in demons or anything supernatural. Such phenomena are surely the result of superstitious ignorance. Therefore, exorcism is irrelevant and they are not asking this question. Others find the question distasteful and they avoid it. Anything supernatural disturbs them, and they do not like being disturbed; they like things under their control. Then there are those who say that Christians today are not called to cast out demons, nor should they ever consider doing so. At the other extreme are fanatics who sincerely believe they are not only possessing the authority to exorcize demons, they see them almost wherever they look. With great bravado they profess to possess the power to confront and cast out demons at will. Enthusiasm, here, is undoubtedly far greater than their enlightenment.

What is the correct answer? Scripture repeatedly reveals that Satan and demons are very active on planet Earth and will do all within their power to destroy the lives of men, women, and even children. The increase in the demonic warfare which begins with Christ's coming into the world has set a pattern for today. Evil forces constantly seek to thwart Christ's work. That is why, especially in times of Christian revival, Satan and his allies are extraordinarily active. Even so, Christians need not fear such attacks, for God rules over all. *'You, dear children, are from God and have overcome them, because the one who is in you is greater than the one who is in the world'* (1 John 4:4). Therefore, does it always follow that Christians are able to confront and conquer demons?

What are Christians to do in a case of suspected demon possession? How is it possible to distinguish a physiological or psychological disorder from demon possession? How can we know who is possessed by demons and who is not? These are difficult questions because the Bible does not provide us with any direct reference. All that we can do is to carefully examine some of the biblical examples of people who suffered from this terrifying problem. Therefore, in what follows, we will examine some of the different symptoms of demonic influence and thus try to gain some insight as to how Satan can affect the lives of men, women and children.

SYMPTOMS OF DEMON POSSESSION

We began this chapter by referring to the man who was possessed by many demons (Mark 5:1–20). This man reveals several common characteristics which are typical of possession. The first fact is that these demons, evil or unclean spirits, call them what you like, actually reside within him. They can control all that he does and says.

People who are possessed by demons may exhibit supernatural strength. In Mark 5:3,4 we are told that the demoniac could not be restrained. Many times people had used chains to tie his hands and feet, but he always broke them off. No one was strong enough to control him. Human power was unable to do anything to control this astonishing supernatural strength. Another demoniac, energized by the strength of a demon, attacked seven itinerant Jewish exorcists. The incantation they used was this: 'In the name of Jesus, whom Paul preaches, I command you to come out' (Acts 19:13). Their use of the name of Jesus as a magic incantation led to disastrous consequences. The demon, who spoke through the mouth of the possessed man, readily acknowledged that he knew Jesus and Paul, but 'who are you?' (Acts 19:15) Instead of this man becoming subdued, the demon possessing him made him even more violent and he turned against them. These exorcists were given such a beating that they fled from the house, naked and badly wounded (Acts 19:16). It's unlikely that they ever tried to exorcize anyone in the name of Jesus again.

We should note that a much worse fate awaits those who use the name of Jesus, which is above every name, without being his. *'Many will say to me on that day, "Lord, Lord, did we not prophesy in your name, and in your name drive out demons and perform many miracles?" Then I will tell them plainly, "I never knew you. Away from me, you evildoers!"'* (Matthew 7:22,23).

A further sign of demon possession is inconsistent and sometimes violent behaviour. The demon-possessed man came to meet Jesus presumably for help (Mark 5:2). Then he suddenly shows fear and begs Jesus not to torture him (v. 7). He also shows great opposition to the things of God: *'What do you want with me … ?'* he yells. Clearly, these demons have taken control of this man's personality. They are able to speak through his mouth and to answer when addressed in a voice that is clearly not his own.

There is also supernatural knowledge – clairvoyance; this man knew who Jesus was even though they had never met before (Mark 5:7). In Acts 16:16–18 we read of a slave girl who had an evil spirit that gave her the ability to know things beyond her own knowledge. She followed Paul and his associates, crying out, *'These men are servants of the Most High God, who are telling you the way to be saved.'* This went on day after day until Paul got so annoyed that he turned and spoke to the demon within her: *'In the name of Jesus Christ I command you to come out of her!'* And instantly it left her. Paul followed the precedent of Jesus, who refused the testimony of demons, even when they spoke the truth (e.g. Mark 1:23–25). Clearly, it is a mistake to believe that Satan and his allies only ever speak lies. If they did, their deceptions would be much easier to detect.

What settles the question, once and for all, of whether or not a person is possessed by a demon is transference. In this instance the many evil spirits came out of the man and went into a herd of about two thousand pigs (Mark 5:11–13). The effect on the man was instantaneous and conspicuous. People who came to see what had happened found him *dressed and in his right mind* (v. 15). Events like this do not ever occur naturally.

Critics of exorcism contend that psychological disorders are often misdiagnosed as demon possession. In such cases, exorcism will not only be ineffective, it may exacerbate the condition and can even be considered abuse. Hence, it is vital to realize that personality changes such as aggression, depression, immodesty, antisocial behaviour and blasphemy may, or may not, have natural explanations. Behavioural abnormality and demon possession are not necessarily synonymous.

Encountering a person inhabited by a demon, or demons, is a very serious matter. Thus, the Christian facing such a situation needs spiritual discernment. Otherwise it can result in tragic consequences. Demons do not always leave quietly. Even with Jesus it was sometimes very noisy, with shrieks and nasty manifestations. Likewise, the modern-day ministry of deliverance is in this respect no different from the ministry of Jesus.

Those who say that anyone can cast out a demon using the name of the Lord Jesus are wrong (Acts 19:13–16). It should be realized that any attempt to make direct contact and converse with an evil spirit is extremely dangerous, regardless of the reason or motive. Some exorcists insist that they will never call anything a demon until they have talked with it. They consider it essential to discover the name of the demon so that they can then cast it out by the more powerful name of Jesus. Other exorcists scoff at this idea. They believe that one ought to be able to command demons to leave immediately.

In the case of the severely demonized man, the Gerasene demoniac, we see that: *'Jesus asked him, "What is your name?" "Legion," he replied, because many demons had gone into him'* (Luke 8:30). This raises an important question that many people's minds struggle with, and that is: Should those involved in healing and deliverance ministries ever talk to demons? In some circumstances, I believe, with severely demonized people it is a necessary part of this ministry. But it must be stressed that any information sought from demons is to be strictly related to the delivery of people from the powers of darkness. To go any further is bordering on mediumship which is absolutely forbidden in the Scriptures (Deuteronomy 18:10–12).

There are exorcists who in a foolhardy way venture into dangerous territory by claiming to possess personal authority and power to recognize, address and control demons. Only the Lord Jesus can do that, and we must never think otherwise. If we are ever confronted by a demoniac, then it is necessary to pray and also to exhort the demoniac to turn to Christ. He alone can act as mediator between God and humanity, for salvation and deliverance. Using any other means leaves us exposed to demonic power.

The supernatural is fascinating, and people naturally find themselves attracted to it. That is why bookstores and libraries have many books on demons, the occult and suchlike. Games, television shows, magazines and films about these subjects are also very popular. For instance, William Peter Blatty's 1971 novel *The Exorcist* and 1973 film by the same name were great moneymakers. They tell the story of a girl named Regan who innocently played with an Ouija board and met a spirit by the name of Captain Howdy. This evil spirit invades the house and eventually invades the girl. There follows an incredible struggle between human lives and demonic forces. Though wrong theologically on many points, Blatty's account contains some truth, maybe because it was based upon a supposedly real event.

In *The Exorcist*, the Ouija – meaning 'yes, yes' (*oui* in French and *ja* in German) – board acts as a means through which Captain Howdy takes possession of Regan. This scene, which is vital to the plot, is brief and easily forgotten, eclipsed by the horror that follows. The necessary lesson to be learned is that through playing with the Ouija board she encountered evil. Pastor H. Richard Neff concludes that primarily the Ouija board works because of autosuggestion, but he also warns: 'A sufficient number of people have got into serious psychological difficulty through the use of a Ouija board to warn us that these instruments may not be "innocent toys." Most serious students of parapsychology strongly advise people not to use Ouija boards and such instruments.'[1]

Numerous personal testimonies, stories on the internet and in literature that describe encounters with spirits through using these boards are readily available.

With some slight variations, the Ouija board is a flat, rectangular board on which are marked the letters from A to Z, the numbers 0 to 9 and the words 'yes', 'no' and 'goodbye'. The message indicator (planchette) is a small heart-shaped table with three legs; sometimes an upturned glass is used. Participants lightly place two fingers on the indicator and it is moved about to spell words in answer to questions. But what makes it work? The general consensus is that it is controlled by the conscious or subconscious mind of the operator, or occasionally from contact with evil spirits. Certainly the revelations often go far beyond what can satisfactorily be explained as coming from the conscious or subconscious mind of the operator.

Following its commercial introduction by Elijah Bond, who filed for the patent in 1890, the Ouija board was regarded as a harmless game. The same is true today. In 1967, the Ouija board was America's favourite board game, surpassing Monopoly, with sales of 2.3 million.[2] That interest waned, but Ouija's popularity is still strong, despite the potential danger. No matter how innocent it may appear, playing with Ouija boards can be an opening for evil spirits to dominate the life of an individual. Moreover, any tools of the occult are things that God has condemned (Leviticus 19:31; 20:6). This is a straightforward command and it requires a straightforward response. Christians must distance themselves from all occult practices and accept that it is wrong to seek spiritual power from somewhere other than God.

CAN A CHRISTIAN EVER BE DEMON POSSESSED?

Whether or not a Christian can be possessed by a demon has been a contentious subject for a long time. So let us turn to the Bible. Although it does not provide us with any direct reference, related biblical truths leave us in no doubt that Christians cannot be possessed or fully controlled by demons. This is because the Holy Spirit indwells every Christian without exception (Romans 8:9; 1 Corinthians 3:16). The apostle John reassuringly says, '*If anyone acknowledges that Jesus is the Son of God, God lives in him and he in God*' (1 John 4:15). A few verses earlier he says to his readers, '*You, dear children, are from God and have overcome them, because the one who is in you is greater than the one who is in the world*' (1 John 4:4). Who is the one in us? It is the Holy Spirit. Who is the one in the world? It is the spirit of the antichrist, 'the spirit of falsehood' (v. 6).

A born again Christian cannot be possessed by a demon. When a person receives Jesus Christ as Lord and Saviour they are translated from the power (or jurisdiction) of Satan to God (see Colossians 1:13). From then on they are rightfully possessed by the Holy Spirit.

It needs to be said, however, that Christians can be oppressed or influenced by demonic powers. The apostle Peter is a good example of a believer who was influenced by the devil (Matthew 16:23). He temporarily became Satan's agent. Furthermore, we must never forget that this was just after he had made the inspired confession, *'You are the Christ, the Son of the living God'* (v. 16). Clearly, someone who can be mightily used by God can equally be used by Satan.

As the author of confusion, Satan finds all kinds of ways to lead people astray. This should be a stern warning to all who are at the forefront of Christian ministry. Committed Christians will be actively involved in warfare against evil spiritual forces, as we shall see in the next chapter.

WHERE DO DEMONS GO WHEN THEY ARE CAST OUT?

The above question is often asked of those involved in deliverance ministry. Do demons that are cast out go to a specific place? Can demons return to the person whom they left? Or can they enter someone else?

There are only a few brief references within the Bible which are helpful in this matter. The first is where Jesus, at the demons' request, dispatched them into a large herd of pigs. On entering the pigs, the whole herd rushed down the steep hillside into the lake and drowned (Mark 5:11-13). But what happened to the demons after that? Certainly, they would not drown. It is possible when they rushed into the lake that they rushed further into the abyss and were imprisoned. We can, however, only speculate because the story focuses upon the victory over demons.

Another reference is the account of Jesus healing the epileptic boy. He not only commands the evil spirit to come out of the boy, but also to *'never enter him again'* (Mark 9:25). This indicates that demonic re-entry is a possibility for some people.

The major references relating to demonic repossession are to be found in Matthew 12:43–45 and Luke 11:24–26. To be delivered from demonic power is a blessing. But for an exorcism to have a lasting, permanent value, it is vital that the Holy Spirit takes the place of the dispatched evil spirit. Otherwise a vacuum will exist which will be an irresistible temptation for the evil spirit to return. In addition it returns with *'seven other spirits more wicked than itself'* (Matthew 12:45; Luke 11:26).

OCCULT PRACTICES

The word 'occult' is derived from the Latin word *occultus*, meaning 'hidden, covered, mysterious or secret things'. It covers a wide range of practices which often pervade society in subtle ways. Those who play with Ouija boards and think it is a game; those who practice palmistry, read tarot cards, tea leaves, coffee grounds, or crystal gazing; those who attempt to contact the spirits of the dead or indulge in psychic phenomena; those who read their horoscopes are examples of people involved with the kingdom of the occult. And it is dangerous because it can open the door to the powers of darkness. Furthermore, in rejecting God there is no defence against Satan and his demons.

Acts 19:18,19 reveals that a number of people in Ephesus who had been deeply influenced by magic were transformed by the power of the Holy Spirit. Convicted of their sin, they confessed their evil deeds. But more than that, they brought their scrolls containing magic spells and incantations and, despite their great monetary value, burned them publicly. They realized their need to completely reject the world of the occult because it was incompatible to a Christian lifestyle.

It is a sad fact that many people become involved, either knowingly or unknowingly, with things that God has condemned. He condemns the person who '*sacrifices his son or daughter in the fire, practices divination or sorcery, interprets omens, engages in witchcraft, or casts spells, or who is a medium or spiritist or who consults the dead. Anyone who does these things is detestable to the LORD*' (Deuteronomy 18:10–12). These evil practices were the cause of God's judgment on the Canaanites, and his attitude has not changed. Therefore, it would be foolish and irresponsible for anyone to repeat these practices which God despises.

The work of a 'medium' or 'spiritist' is among the list of occupations forbidden by God. Spiritualism is a belief that the spirits of the dead have the ability and the inclination to communicate with the living, especially through mediums. It is necessary to say at the outset, in discussing this phenomenon, that the term 'spiritism' rather than 'Spiritualism' is regarded by some mediums as being abusive. The former is a nickname given to the Spiritual Church Movement by its opponents.

Spiritualism has several features that are common to Christianity. Examples of this are Sunday services, the singing of hymns, and a belief in life after death. There are, however, significant differences. For instance, the Bible is not considered to be the fundamental source of knowledge about God and the afterlife. Their personal contact with spirits provides that. Neither do they accept that Jesus Christ is 'the only name' under heaven by which a person can be saved (see Acts 4:12). He is considered to be a prophet, teacher, medium and healer. They believe that heaven and hell are not places to which we are destined to go, but instead states of mind of our own creation.

Modern Spiritualism is generally considered to date from events which happened in Hydesville, New York on 31 March 1848. Two sisters, Margaret and Kate Fox, claimed to have established contact with a spirit entity. News of this quickly spread and provided a great impetus for the advancement of Spiritualism. Margaret later confessed that what they had done was a hoax, and though she tried to recant her confession, their reputation was destroyed. The same could not be said of Spiritualism. This worldwide religion has many churches affiliated to various organizations, while others remain independent.

Of course, the belief that a person may communicate with those who have died is not new. The Old Testament makes reference to it on several occasions (Leviticus 19:31; Deuteronomy 18:11). There is also the record of Saul's visit to the woman at Endor, which resulted in the departed Samuel speaking to him (1 Samuel 28). When Saul saw the size of the Philistine army, he was terrified. Hence, he contacted a woman who was a medium. He visited her incognito and asked what he should do. The woman realized that what he asked was forbidden in Israel (1 Samuel 28:9). Saul himself had, at some point in his reign, '*expelled the mediums and spiritists from the land*' (v. 3). In spite of that, Saul reassured her that nothing bad would happen and so she agreed. '*Then the woman asked, "Whom shall I bring up for you?" "Bring up Samuel," he said*' (v. 11).

Then something occurred that is unprecedented in the Bible. God permitted Samuel to return. Spiritualists will usually claim that this medium materialized Samuel, but that is false. She probably intended to materialize something Saul would believe was Samuel and failed. Instead, to her terrified amazement,

Samuel actually appeared! This was not a vision of the prophet. Neither, was it Satan or demons masquerading as Samuel. The text is unmistakably clear. It does not refer to 'one who had the appearance of Samuel'. It says '*Samuel said to Saul*' (v. 15). Here we have a real and unparalleled appearance of the glorified spirit of Samuel. This is the only séance ever mentioned in the Bible and it ended with a pronouncement of judgment. Saul would be defeated by the Philistines.

People are attracted to Spiritualism for various reasons. The possibility of communicating with a departed loved one is a primary attraction. Spiritualist healing meetings have also attracted large crowds. Still other people, often dissatisfied with materialistic lifestyles, are attracted by curiosity of the supernatural.

Spiritualists would claim that manifestations are due to contact with departed spirits. On the other hand, Christians would see them either as chicanery, psychic force, or that the spirits contacted are not those of the dead but rather fallen angels (demons) who impersonate the dead and fool those who seek them. That is why the Bible leaves us in no doubt that we are never to try to make contact with those who have died.

The Bible reveals everything that we need to know about our future. Yet a vast number of people consult their horoscope every day. They believe that the stars and the planets have a decisive influence on the destiny of human life. As a result impersonal cosmic forces take precedence over the God who created the sun, moon and stars. For some people astrology has become a religion. Christians, however, reject astrology, fortune-telling, spiritualism and the like to guide them; their walk of faith and future are in the hands of God.

THE INFILTRATION OF THE OCCULT INTO
THE CHURCH TODAY

Today there are numerous voices seeking our attention, and many cults attracting widespread support. We should not be surprised by this. *'For the time will come when men will not put up with sound doctrine. Instead, to suit their own desires, they will gather around them a great number of teachers to say what their itching ears want to hear. They will turn their ears away from the truth and turn aside to myths'* (2 Timothy 4:3–5). These people are more interested in the sensational, in signs and wonders, than they are in obeying the sober Word of God. They corrupt the church's true mission, which is to proclaim the good news of salvation in Christ.

The aim of Satan is to lead people astray, and so he readily promotes all practices which are selfish and sensual. Unbiblical ideas have infiltrated many – especially extreme charismatic – churches. There are preachers to whom the Bible has become practically irrelevant. They claim that God speaks to them by direct revelation through dreams and visions so as to authenticate their particular doctrine. Their impressive declarations offering supernatural experiences, health, wealth and orgies of ecstasy are appealing. Some of these preachers are not easily perceived as false, for what they do is to mix their own ideas with spiritual truth. They freely talk about God. They talk about the grace of God. They talk about Jesus. They falsely claim to have been sent by God. As a result there are many impressionable people who unwittingly indulge in liberal practices that are contrary to Christ's standards. For instance, mystical meditation, chanting, wild dancing, uncontrollable laughter, shrieking and sobbing, and banal, repetitive singing, are fraught with potential dangers. Why anyone would consider that such practices manifest God's power is difficult to comprehend: *'The fruit of the Spirit is ... self-*

control' (Galatians 5:22,23). Indeed, any practice based upon self-willed feelings rather than faith will not glorify God and thus be offensive to him.

In 1 John 4:1, Christians are instructed to *'not believe every spirit, but test the spirits to see whether they are from God, because many false prophets have gone out into the world'*. Numerous other references could be quoted, indicating the need to expose those involved in the cults, the occult and other religions. We cannot ignore the fact that practices which distort the central message of Christianity, many from Eastern and African countries, have infiltrated some churches and present a serious challenge. For instance, the New Age movement is a mixture of Eastern spirituality and occult ideas. Transcendental meditation, spiritualism, Freemasonry, witchcraft and perversions of biblical truth, all forbidden territory to Christians, present a real challenge to those who are true believers in Christ. Such false teachings must be rejected and refuted.

Those who expose doctrinal error are often described as divisive and as not showing Christian love. Nevertheless, we are called to fight the good fight. It should be noted that the fight is against false ideas and practices inside the church, not outside. Jesus said: *'Watch out for false prophets. They come to you in sheep's clothing, but inwardly they are ferocious wolves. By their fruit you will recognize them'* (Matthew 7:15,16a). It is that which distinguishes the children of God from the children of Satan. False teachers, who claim that they have been sent by God but have not, come in many subtle guises. Hence, they appear to be harmless and gifted, telling people what they want to hear. False teachers will claim, 'You can have everything you want now.' Nothing could be further from the truth. Invariably their corrupt influence of encouraging people to live for the present, not for the future, will have awful consequences. We need to be constantly alert against all teachers who falsely promise us a life free from problems, pain and persecution (2 Timothy 3:12).

The difference between false and true teachers is great and this difference will, sooner or later, be seen in their works. True teachers are commissioned by God and will uphold sound doctrine and holy living. In sharp contrast, false teachers lack divine authority, they are representatives of Satan masquerading as angels of light, and they will lead people astray from the paths of godliness. The grace of God becomes a licence for immorality, and the divine authority of Jesus Christ, who has absolute sovereignty, is renounced (Jude 4).

So what should we do in such situations? The answer is that we need to be on our guard against any who teach things which are contrary to the true character of God. The only defence against false teaching and the powers of evil is to put on the full armour of God described in Ephesians 6:10–18, otherwise we will be ignominiously defeated. Our only authority as to what is doctrinal truth or error must be the invincible sword of the Spirit, which is the entire Word of God.

NOTES

1. H. Richard Neff, *Psychic Phenomena and Religion* (Philadelphia: Westminster, 1971), p. 131.

2. See Edmond C. Gruss, *Cults and the Occult* 4th ed. (Phillipsburg, NJ: P&R Publishing, 2002), p. 174. Gruss obtained his information by letter from Parker Brothers' consumer relations advisor Evelyn Cusco, 5 May 1992. The patents on the board were purchased in 1966 by Parker Brothers.

CHAPTER 7

SPIRITUAL WARFARE

When Jesus, during his time on earth, preached about the kingdom of heaven, he invaded the territory of another kingdom, the kingdom of Satan. By calling him *'the prince of this world'* (John 12:31), Jesus acknowledged Satan's ruling authority over evil. In another text, Satan is called *'The god of this age'* because he is the embodiment of all ungodliness in this world (2 Corinthians 4:4). Satan is the constant arch enemy of God and so is diametrically opposed to all biblical truth. Satan and his fallen angelic followers are always eager in their attempts to destroy humankind and defeat God's kingdom on earth. Satan is the reason for the aggressiveness of evil in our world today.

Christians live in enemy occupied territory and therefore experience, to a certain extent, what Christ experienced. The Christian life is a battle against evil powers and principalities; it is not a life of ease and undisturbed tranquility. If we follow Christ our life will not be a bed of roses, it will be a crown of thorns.

As Paul reminds us, '... *everyone who wants to live a godly life in Christ Jesus will be persecuted*' (2 Timothy 3:12). The emphasis here is to be placed on '*everyone*' (not some) and '*will be persecuted*'. Paul's experience is by no means unique. Everyone who intently serves God is bound to attract Satan's attention again and again, because they are a threat to his kingdom. For this reason the Bible repeatedly warns us about the reality of spiritual war and its consequences.

In Ephesians 6:12 Paul provides a detailed and daunting description of the invisible forces arrayed against us. '*For our struggle is not against flesh and blood,*' he writes, '*but against the rulers, against the authorities, against the powers of this dark world and against the spiritual forces of evil in the heavenly realms.*' These formidable enemies should never be ignored, minimized or trivialized, because to do so is to court disaster.

It is very clear that the major problem for the Christian is warfare not against human beings who oppose Christ, but rather against mighty spiritual forces intent on destroying God's redemptive work. Thus, this raises the urgent question: How can any of us face such a powerful adversary whose power vastly exceeds our own? It would appear to be an impossible task.

Although a mighty opponent, Satan and the spiritual forces of evil are not able to stand before the power of God. There are many things that Satan cannot do. Satan is potent but, unlike God, he is not omnipotent. That being so, we need not despair. The Holy Spirit that dwells within Christians is greater than the spirit of the antichrist. Hence, if God is for us, it matters not who is against us. The sixteenth-century Scottish reformer John Knox is often credited with saying, 'A man with God is always in the majority.'[1] But it must be emphasized that we cannot withstand any satanic power without the Father, Son and Holy

Spirit. Other than God himself, a more powerful spirit than Satan does not exist.

The rebellion that Satan began in heaven is an ongoing battle against both God and humanity. There is a spiritual conflict raging here and now between the kingdom of God and the kingdom of evil. Moreover, there will be no cessation of hostilities, not even a temporary break, until Satan and his underlings are defeated once and for all.

Throughout history, from Genesis to Revelation, Satan is active. In answer to God's inquiry, *'Where have you come from?'* Satan replied, *'From roaming through the earth and going to and fro in it'* (Job 1:7). Satan is represented as restless, ruthless and relentless. His activities are to put people, in particular God's servants, to the test. Because of this it is not surprising that Peter gives us a stern warning. He portrays Satan as a prowling, roaring lion looking for someone to devour (1 Peter 5:8). Peter had experienced the personal cost of battling against such a formidable enemy. The warning here is very clear: *'Be self-controlled and alert.'* Be on your guard! One of the greatest crimes of a soldier is to fall asleep while on duty.

EARTHLY REBELLION

Spiritual warfare on earth began when Satan appeared to Eve as a serpent and tempted her to take the forbidden fruit. As a consequence, the first human beings, Adam and Eve, were separated from their Creator. Ever since then, Satan has been constantly active in trying to drive a wedge between God and his people.

Satan influenced King David, the godly leader of ancient Israel, to sin. For example, in 1 Chronicles 21:1, we are told that: *'Satan rose up against Israel and incited David to take a census of Israel.'* David, during his time of power and prosperity, is forgetting that his strength came entirely from his faith in God. He ignored the advice of his military commander, Joab, who could see the danger of David's pride and self-sufficient attitude. He knew no blessing would come through counting the fighting men of the nation. Joab, although not a great spiritual man, was correct. David soon realized that he had done a very foolish thing and asked God to forgive him.

In the New Testament, we see that Peter recognized the subtle hand of Satan in the deadly crime of Ananias and Sapphira. He challenged Ananias: *'Ananias, how is it that Satan has so filled your heart that you have lied to the Holy Spirit and have kept for yourself some of the money you received for the land?'* (Acts 5:3). His sin is not only a lie but also theft. That, however, is not the whole story. If their hypocrisy had been tolerated, it would have seriously affected the development of Christianity in its infancy. Even the apostle Peter, as we saw in chapter 6, could become a mouthpiece of Satan.

Whenever Christ's church stands uncompromisingly against the world, then persecution is the inevitable result. The reason for this is obvious. Anyone who lives a godly life in Christ Jesus will be different. For this reason the godly always arouse the antagonism of the worldly. These worldly opponents not only disagree, they react with hatred and animosity. Why? It is because, whether they realize it or not, they are influenced by Satan. That is what the Bible teaches us. Christ said: 'If the world hates you, keep in mind that it hated me first. If you belonged to the world, it would love you as its own. As it is, you do not belong to the world, but I have chosen you out of the world. That is why the world hates you. Remember the words I spoke to you: 'No servant is greater than his master.' If they persecuted me, they will persecute you also ...' (John 15:18–20; cf. 16:33)

Satan will do everything within his power to prevent the development of the kingdom of God. Thus, for example, Paul had his plans interfered with and was prevented by Satan from doing what he wanted to do. To the Thessalonians, he wrote: *'For we wanted to come to you – certainly I, Paul, did, again and again – but Satan stopped us'* (1 Thessalonians 2:18). How did Satan achieve this? We do not know the details. Moreover, it does not matter. What is primarily important for us to remember is that Satan succeeded; but only because this was in accord with God's plan concerning the work Paul was to do.

The church in Smyrna experienced severe suffering because of the power of Satan. Christians were slandered by those who, according to Christ's own words, *'say they are Jews and are not, but are a synagogue of Satan'* (Revelation 2:9). But that is not all. There is a warning of worse trials to come, and encouragements to endure: *'Do not be afraid of what you are about to suffer. I tell you, the devil will put some of you in prison to test you, and you will suffer persecution for ten days. Be faithful, even to the point of death, and I will give you the crown of life'* (v. 10). These Christians would be imprisoned on false charges by so-called Jews who were in league with Satan. In this instance we have a picture of a battle between the power of God and the forces of evil.

It should be realized that Satan can only make us transgress the commands of God if we are willing to collaborate. Therefore we should never attempt to evade responsibility for our actions by placing the blame onto Satan or others. Adam tried to mitigate his guilt after he ate the forbidden fruit. He said, *'The woman you put here with me – she gave me some fruit from the tree, and I ate it'* (Genesis 3:12). Rather than admit obvious guilt he tried to blame his wife and, by imputation, he blamed God for putting her at his side. Like Adam, Eve also had an excuse; she accused the serpent of deceiving her and by doing so also blamed God. Certainly God is sovereign over all of his creatures and their actions. Yet we cannot blame him for any wrongdoing. It is impossible to evade the guilt of our sins for, like the angels, we were created responsible beings that will be held accountable before God.

RECOGNIZING THE ENEMY

Throughout the Bible, the writers are aware that in this world there is a mighty power of evil. Sometimes that power is named Satan, sometimes the devil. It is clear whatever we might call him, that our major fight is not with human beings but against demonic forces. How, then, can we ever expect to resist the attacks of such formidable enemies?

Before going into any battle, it is wise to identify the enemy so as to be prepared. Paul was able to write, '... we are not unaware of his [Satan's] schemes' (2 Corinthians 2:11). In this instance, Paul encouraged a spirit of forgiveness as a means against Satan's entrance into our lives. The overall lesson is that to be forewarned, by knowing the methods that Satan has used in the past, is to be forearmed, and that in itself is a major part of the battle. However, to identify the enemy is often easier said than done. If Satan came to me as a red imp with horns and a forked tail and tried to tempt me I should recognize him immediately, and I would say, 'Get behind me, Satan.' But Satan does not appear in that guise. Our enemy masquerades as an angel of light. He can roar like a lion, but he can also be as subtle as a serpent. He is an expert in every aspect of deceit. If his seductive temptations fail he can attack us with the fierceness of a lion. It is not surprising, therefore, that we need to be prepared for any eventuality that may arise. Preparation and protection are indispensable to winning spiritual battles.

Satan's worst activity is to prevent people from accepting the good news of Christ. While talking about the wheat and the weeds, Jesus explained the unnoticed but powerful influence the 'enemy', who in this story is none other than Satan, wields to neutralize the Word of God (Matthew 13:24–29,36–43). The apostle Paul was well aware of this from experience when he wrote: *The god of this age has blinded the minds of unbelievers, so that they cannot see the light of the gospel of the glory of Christ, who is the image of God'* (2 Corinthians 4:4).

Satan's tactics are the same now as they were in the Garden of Eden. He questions the accuracy of God's Word and creates doubts in our minds. Satan also tries to discourage us, he tells us that we cannot succeed, that the way is far too difficult and the burden much too heavy. He tries to persuade us that we are weak and incapable of victory. On the other hand, Satan can instil in us a feeling of self-importance and self-confidence so that we forget that our strength comes from our faith in God – and such an attitude, of course, always leads to disaster. How many have fallen because of pride! Whatever method Satan uses, his aim is always to cause utter confusion and chaos in the work of God.

All Christians have to face the ongoing battle against God's enemy and theirs. And for this, the strength of the Lord and the full armour of God are the two essentials. Spiritual warfare must always be fought with spiritual weapons. To be armed with God's power is the only way to avoid defeat.

Although the Bible refers to spiritual warfare in several places, it is Paul who primarily addresses the problem in Ephesians 6:10–20. He describes the Christian as a soldier both in character and conduct. These verses must be carefully studied and fully obeyed, for only then is victory assured.

THE FULL ARMOUR OF GOD

In 1655, the Puritan minister William Gurnall published his treatise *The Christian in Complete Armour*. The eighth edition of 1821 consists of three volumes, two hundred and sixty-one chapters and one thousand four hundred and seventy-two pages for an exposition of eleven verses (Ephesians 6:10–20). Although extremely verbose, it is certainly a classic on spiritual warfare and of great value. It has been republished many times, and revised and abridged versions are available in contemporary English. This is a profoundly biblical book and as relevant and thought-provoking today as it was when first written.

Martyn Lloyd-Jones' two volumes entitled *The Christian Warfare*[2] and *The Christian Soldier*[3] more concisely cover the same eleven verses. These compilations of edited sermons preached on Sunday mornings in Westminster Chapel, London, are an invaluable guide. Lloyd-Jones thoroughly discusses the call to battle, the whole armour of God, and many other practical aspects of our struggle against the forces of darkness.

Paul begins his concluding exhortation with respect to the church's fight against the spiritual forces of evil by saying: *'Finally, be strong in the Lord and in his mighty power'* (Ephesians 6:10). Throughout the Bible we see God's inexhaustible power in operation. Indeed, it is impossible to become a Christian without the power of God's Spirit working within us. Then, too, the Spirit's power is necessary for Christian service; otherwise we shall labour in vain. Do we have that power? Or are we discouraged and sometimes feel like giving up?

Zerubbabel, who was in charge of the rebuilding of the Temple, viewed the task before him as impossible. Then the angel of the LORD spoke to him through the prophet Zechariah: *'"Not by might [the strength of many combined] nor by power* [that of one person], *but by my Spirit,"* says the LORD *Almighty'* (Zechariah 4:6). Zerubbabel still had to work, but God himself would provide him with the necessary power.

Without the Holy Spirit's aid, nothing of any real worth can ever be accomplished. But if God is for us, it matters not who is against us. That is why Paul could say, *'I can do everything through him who gives me strength'* (Philippians 4:13). Paul had the strength for whatever tribulation or persecution he might face, and that experience can be ours. We need to be strong with the Lord's mighty power. How we need to pray for an outpouring of God's Spirit upon his church today!

But what does it mean to be strong in the Lord? Does a large active church membership and abundant material resources necessarily indicate signs of spiritual strength? Of course not! The members of the church in Laodicea were deluded by believing that they were self-sufficient; they either disbelieved or forgot how powerful their spiritual enemies were, and thought they could manage without God. Spiritually this church was *'wretched, pitiful, poor, blind and naked'* (Revelation 3:17). This is a sharp contrast to the church in Smyrna which was very poor in natural wealth but rich in faith (Revelation 2:9). Their great treasure was in heaven.

The true strength of any church is dependent entirely upon the holiness of its members. Their mark of true spirituality is not assertion but submission to each other (Ephesians 5:21) and to God. They are conscious of their own weakness, the power of the enemy, and their dependence upon the power of the Lord. Those who lead must be sensitive to the promptings of the Holy Spirit, responding by faith as he leads.

Ephesians 6:10 taken in isolation could give the impression that all our battles are fought for us. 'Let go and let God' is a phrase used in some gatherings, but is it biblical? Should we just stand back and wait for it all to be done for us? *'Moses answered the people, 'Do not be afraid. Stand firm and you will see the deliverance the* LORD *will bring you today. The Egyptians you see today you will never see again. The* LORD *will fight for you; you need only to be still'* (Exodus 14:13,14). In this instance they do not have to defend themselves or fight. Usually, however, soldiers do not achieve victory by doing nothing, nor can a Christian win the overall battle without strenuous effort. That is why Paul speaks about being *'able to stand your ground'* (Ephesians 6:13), but first it is essential to put on the full armour of God. Further, he says that as Christians we can *'extinguish all the flaming arrows of the evil one'* (v. 16), but only if we *'take up the shield of faith'.* James says, *'Resist the devil, and he will flee from you'* (James 4:7), but only if we submit ourselves to God. This principle is often taught in the Bible. There is to be a combination of divine enabling and human participation in Christian warfare. Only then is victory assured.

In spiritual warfare it is necessary to put on the full armour of God. Omit nothing *'so that when the day of evil comes* [that is, the day of severe trial]*, you may be able to stand your ground'* (Ephesians 6:13). Nothing, other than the full armour of God, is ever adequate in this awful conflict in which we are actively involved. That is why we are told twice to put on the full armour (vv. 11,13). To leave any part of our body exposed would lead to disaster, for the enemy will always attack at our most vulnerable point.

Some commentators state that in Paul's description of this armour there is no reference to protection for the back. This, they believe, is indicative of the fact that Christians should never retreat for to do so would expose an unprotected area. However, the soldier's breastplate often protected his back as well as his front and thus provided adequate protection. Even so, Christians must not take a backward step to any assault.

Paul was well acquainted with Roman soldiers. He encountered many on his journeys. It is not surprising, therefore, that he would think of their armour and liken it to the spiritual armour that the soldier of Christ must wear. He was probably also influenced by his knowledge of the Old Testament. For example, Isaiah 59:17 describes how God put on righteousness as his breastplate and placed the helmet of salvation on his head. These various pieces of equipment are now given to the church. In this sense they are truly the armour of God, and each piece is essential in our fight against the spiritual forces of evil. Hence, Paul issues the following mobilization order so that we might win the battle against the devil's schemes:

> Stand firm then, with the belt of truth buckled round your waist,
> with the breastplate of righteousness in place, and with your
> feet fitted with the readiness that comes from the gospel of peace.
> In addition to all this, take up the shield of faith, with which you
> can extinguish all the flaming arrows of the evil one. Take the
> helmet of salvation and the sword of the Spirit, which is
> the word of God.

(Ephesians 6:14–17)

The translation 'full armour' is in the Greek a single word, *panoplia*, which may be transliterated as 'panoply'. We have an example of this in Charles Wesley's hymn 'Soldiers of Christ, Arise':

> But take, to arm you for the fight,
> the panoply of God.[4]

The *panoplia* was the complete equipment used by heavily armed infantry.

Our first piece of equipment to which Paul refers is the 'belt of truth' (v. 14). This belt, tightly buckled round the waist, was vital because it bound together any long and loose garments that people wore. Otherwise they would have been a hindrance to any vigorous action. The Israelites, at the time of the first Passover, as they waited to make their escape from Egypt were prepared with their cloaks tucked into their belts (Exodus 12:11). This was customary practice when a person had to move quickly. Another example is when Elijah prepared to outrun on foot the horse-drawn chariot of Ahab by *'tucking his cloak into his belt'* (1 Kings 18:46).

Truth is the Christian's belt. But what is meant here by this word 'truth'? Some people understand this to mean the truth of the Scriptures. Others, however, believe that Paul is referring to truth in the sense of sincerity of mind and heart. Whichever way we look at it, one is not acceptable without the other. God requires *'truth in the inner parts'* (Psalm 51:6).

The second piece of equipment is *'the breastplate of righteousness'* (v. 14). This breastplate was worn to protect such vital organs as heart and lungs, and no soldier at that time would go into battle without one. Righteousness, which is provided by God himself, is to be the Christian's breastplate. No righteousness of our own would be adequate because it is always imperfect. But to have a righteous relationship with God through Christ spells victory.

Next, the Christian must have feet shod with *'the gospel of peace'* (v. 15). But what does this mean? Some people say that the Christian soldier is the messenger of the gospel, and that the footwear speaks of the Christian's readiness to go and announce the gospel message of peace and salvation to others. It seems to me, however, that

Paul's main thought here is not evangelization; rather it is the ability of the soldier to stand firm against the enemy.

The Roman soldier wore footwear with heavy studded soles that gave him a firm foothold without impeding his mobility. But how is it possible for a Christian to stand firm in the battle? Surely it is because those who experience within their heart the peace of God, which the gospel proclaims, have been relieved of a tremendous burden. Thus, their belief in the gospel and the assurance it gives enables them to remain steadfast and confident in battle.

The fourth piece of equipment is 'the shield of faith' (v. 16). This is not the small round shield, but the large oblong one measuring about 1.2 metres by 0.75, which protected the whole body from attack. At that time, soldiers often dipped their darts or arrows in pitch or similar material, lit them, and then fired them burning against their enemy. Hence, to extinguish these fiery missiles, the shields were covered with non-inflammable leather.

What, then, are we to understand by 'all the flaming arrows of the evil one', and what is the shield with which Christians can protect themselves? Undoubtedly Satan's arsenal contains many kinds of flaming arrows. Some of these will inflame doubt, others envy, greed, lust, pride and suchlike. Only by faith, utter confidence in the power and protection of God, can the Christian fully extinguish every temptation. God 'is a shield to those who take refuge in him' (Proverbs 30:5), and it is by faith that we turn to him for protection. Faith links us to God's peace and power.

The faith shield is followed by 'the helmet of salvation' (v. 17). In 1 Thessalonians 5:8, Paul identified the helmet with the hope of salvation. Here, in Ephesians, it is salvation itself. This difference is easily explained since salvation, although an inheritance not yet fully acquired in this life, is a privilege the Christian already enjoys. Therefore, this confident awareness of full salvation, because of the resurrection of Christ, is the foundation of hope. Our head will always be protected while such hope is its helmet.

The sixth and final piece of equipment to be described is 'the sword' (v. 17). This is the only one of the six capable of clearly being used for attack as well as defence. That being so, in this instance the English word 'armour' can be misleading. We tend to think of armour as a defensive covering, usually of metal, to protect the body. But the Greek word *panoplia* has no such limitation.

This weapon is the short sword (machaira) with which the soldier could either defend himself or engage in close personal combat. The Christian, who is also involved in such combat, is to fight with 'the sword of the Spirit' which is then further identified as 'the word of God'. All Scripture is given by the Spirit (2 Timothy 3:16; see 2 Peter 1:21) and it is applied to our heart by the Spirit.

The Lord himself used this weapon in the wilderness. 'It is written', he said following each of Satan's attacks (Matthew 4:4,7,10). His use of the Scriptures put an end to every argument. Christians need a weapon that can defeat such a powerful foe, and this is it. In 1521, Martin Luther was called before Holy Roman Emperor Charles V at the Diet of Worms (diet meaning a formal meeting, and Worms being a city south of Frankfurt). Luther had criticized the beliefs of the established church and, when challenged, refused to recant. This is the answer that he gave in Worms: 'Unless I am convinced by the testimony of the Scriptures or by clear reason (for I do not trust either in the pope or in councils alone, since it is well known that they have often erred and contradicted themselves), I am bound by the Scriptures I have quoted and my conscience is captive to the Word of God. I cannot and will not retract anything, since it is neither safe nor right to go against conscience.'[5] Every Christian must be able to say the same.

These, then, are the six essential pieces which, combined, constitute the full armour of God: the belt of truth and the breastplate of righteousness, the gospel footwear and the shield of faith, the helmet of salvation and the Spirit's sword. Paul then adds prayer to the list: *'And pray in the Spirit on all occasions with all kinds of prayers and requests. With this in mind, be alert and always keep on praying for all the saints'* (v. 18).

THE IMPORTANCE OF PRAYER

Prayer is not strictly another part of the Christian's armour, as is sometimes suggested, but it is clearly connected with it. How can a Christian be strong in the Lord? The answer is by putting on the full armour of God, and by persistent prayer. Each piece of armour must be put on with prayer. Prayer is to permeate all that we do. It was a realization of this truth that moved William Cowper to write:

Restraining prayer, we cease to fight;
prayer makes the Christian's armour bright;
and Satan trembles when he sees
the weakest saint upon his knees.[6]

Sometimes the question is asked, 'Does prayer change things?' Yes, it certainly does. Yet, even more than things, prayer changes people. To enter God's presence transforms us. The face of Moses was radiant after he met with God (Exodus 34:35). And if we are going to let our light shine before people, so that they might give glory to God, then we must speak to God in prayer. It is prayer that makes the Christian's armour bright. There is nothing that

Satan dreads as much as real, persistent, fervent prayer. He will do everything within his power to prevent people seeking the unconquerable help of God himself.

How should we pray? Paul says that we are to pray in the Spirit. This means to pray with an awareness of God which the Spirit provides; it means to pray in the knowledge that the Spirit helps us in our weakness and even intercedes for us when we cannot find the right words to express ourselves. Sometimes we do not even know what we should pray for. Elijah did not understand what he was asking for when he prayed that he might die (1 Kings 19:4). Neither did Paul when he pleaded with the Lord three times to have the thorn in his flesh removed (2 Corinthians 12:8). Here the Spirit prays against him. He needed that thorn to keep him humble. Thank God for not granting us all that we request of him. '*We do not know what we ought to pray for, but the Spirit himself intercedes for us with groans that words cannot express*' (Romans 8:26). The Spirit prays on our behalf for our well-being in accordance with God's will.

What should we pray for? Some people are continually asking for things and nothing else. But prayer is much more than making requests. Within the Bible there are recorded many different kinds of prayer. Adoration enables us to praise God. Confession of sin provides the way to forgiveness and restoration. Seeking guidance and waiting for his leading. Thanksgiving for God's many blessings, as well as intercession for others plus petitions for ourselves are important aspects of prayer. These prayers may be expressed silently or audibly; often privately but also corporately, and they are our means of communicating with God. Moreover, prayer will increasingly become a part of our character as we grow to be more like Jesus.

A Christian soldier must be constantly alert. When Jesus

went with his disciples to a place called Gethsemane, he knew that Satan was seeking an opportunity to overpower them. Consequently, he said that they should not sleep but should *'Watch and pray'* (Matthew 26:41). The disciples failed to obey this order, which led to disloyalty. For instance, Peter denied knowing Jesus three times just as Jesus had prophesied. Peter had fallen asleep three times in Gethsemane and later three times denied knowing Jesus. We need to be alert at all times, for Satan loves to catch us unawares.

Sometimes we pray for help yet there is no immediate answer. Elijah experienced this when praying for rain: *'And Elijah said to Ahab, "Go, eat and drink, for there is the sound of heavy rain." So Ahab went off to eat and drink, but Elijah climbed to the top of Carmel, bent down to the ground and put his face between his knees. "Go and look towards the sea," he told his servant. And he went up and looked. "There is nothing there," he said. Seven times Elijah said, "Go back." The seventh time the servant reported, "A cloud as small as a man's hand is rising from the sea." So Elijah said, "Go and tell Ahab, 'Hitch up your chariot and go down before the rain stops you.' Meanwhile, the sky grew black with clouds, the wind rose, a heavy rain came on and Ahab rode off to Jezreel'* (1 Kings 18:41–45).

Between any prayer and the answer lies the sovereignty of God. He will act only when he is ready. Christians must persevere in prayer, not only for themselves but for all their fellow believers. As Christians we serve the same God, are involved in the same battle, and by grace and through faith in Jesus Christ are destined to receive the same glory.

A lecturer once asked a student if she could summarize Revelation in one sentence. The student replied, 'Certainly, that's easy.' Somewhat surprised but interested, the lecturer asked for the answer. 'Jesus wins,' she replied.

Jesus is the victor. Satan is a defeated being and his days are numbered. Meanwhile, Christians have a fight to be fought with an unseen enemy who is powerful and deceptive. But by using the armour and weapons God supplies, we are able to win. Christians are to fight in his power and strength, confident and secure in his sovereignty and care. That is our only hope.

NOTES

1. Hannah Ward, Jennifer Wild, *The Lion Christian Quotation Collection* (Oxford: Lion, 1997).

2. Martyn Lloyd-Jones, *The Christian Warfare* (Edinburgh: Banner of Truth Trust, 1976).

3. Martyn Lloyd-Jones, *The Christian Soldier* (Edinburgh: Banner of Truth Trust, 1977).

4. Charles Wesley (1707–78), 'Soldiers of Christ, Arise'.

5. Bernhard Lohse, *Martin Luther: An Introduction to His Life and Work* (Philadelphia, PA: Fortress Press, 1986).

6. William Cowper (1731–1800), 'What Various Hindrances We Meet'.